*The look in the youngsters'
faces as they saw this monster
who might have stepped out
of a fairy tale go up in smoke.
That is a reason for Zozobra.
He appeals to the childish
fancy – in all of us.
It is a scene from a fairy tale
of our own making.*

- Will Shuster

ZOZOBRA & Santa Fe
1924 - 2024

100 Years of Burning Gloom and Loving a Monster in The City Different

Written and Designed by Daniel Clavio

Foreword by Ray Sandoval, Zozobra Event Chair
Contributions by: Congresswoman Teresa Leger Fernández, Andrew Lovato, Judith Moir

*Dedicated to the creative and generous spirit of Will Shuster, Jr.,
to the Zozobradores who build and burn the amazing giant effigy each year,
and to all Santa Feans who love that crazy Gloom Monster. Que Viva!*

Published by The Kiwanis Club of Santa Fe
PO Box 622, Santa Fe, New Mexico 87504
www.BurnZozobra.com

in Association with Direct Currents Publishing, Santa Fe, NM

ISBN: 9798333401984

Summary: *A profusely illustrated comprehensive history of the annual Burning of Zozobra event in
Santa Fe, New Mexico. Started in 1924 as an "alternative Fiesta," 2024 marked the Zozobra Centennial,
the 100-year anniversary of the cherished cultural tradition in which the giant effigy Old Man Gloom is burned.*

The Kiwanis Club of Santa Fe (KCSF), New Mexico, is a volunteer organization that produces the annual Burning of Zozobra to raise funds in support of the youth of Santa Fe. Since 1964, the KCSF has held the exclusive copyright and trademarks to the tradition, which is the Club's major fundraiser. KCSF is affiliated with Kiwanis International, a global organization of volunteers dedicated to improving the world one child and one community at a time.

Net profits from this book support the Preservation of the Burning of Zozobra fund, a 501(c)(3)
dedicated to ensuring the Zozobra tradition will continue to burn brightly long into Santa Fe's future.

*The Kiwanis Club of Santa Fe and the Author would like to express our deepest gratitude to our event volunteers, the community of Santa Fe,
the City of Santa Fe Leadership and Staff, and to the many people and organizations who provided invaluable support for this book,
including: The Santa Fe New Mexican newspaper; the Museum of New Mexico (NM Museum of Art, NM History Museum, Palace of the
Governors), NM Department of Cultural Affairs; New Mexico Magazine, NM Tourism Department; and the Shuster Family. Thank You!
Additional thanks to the Official Zozobra Photographers: Melinda Herrera, Bryce Risley, Marcos Herrera, Aaron Newsom, Andres Maestas.*

Photo Credits: Front Cover: Melinda Herrera. Preceding Page: Michael Heller, Courtesy Palace of the Governors Photo Archives
(NMHM/DCA), #HP.2014.14.1940. Opposite Page: Courtesy Palace of the Governors Photo Archives (NMHM/DCA), #047328.

ZOZOBRA

& Santa Fe

1924 - 2024

100 Years of Burning Gloom
and Loving a Monster in The City Different

Daniel Clavio

Foreword

Zozobra 100: A Century of Flames and Festivities

Welcome to the visual journey through a century of flames, festivity, and the enduring spirit of Zozobra! As the Zozobra Event Chairman and a passionate advocate for this iconic event, it is my pleasure to present to you the Zozobra 100 photo book, capturing the essence of this unique tradition that has captivated hearts and minds for generations.

For a hundred years, Zozobra has stood as a symbol of catharsis, renewal, and community unity. Born out of the creative vision of artist Will Shuster in 1924, Zozobra has evolved from a small gathering to a grand spectacle that lights up the night sky with its fiery glow. Each year, as the towering marionette is set ablaze, we release our worries, fears, and troubles into the flames, making space for new beginnings and fresh perspectives.

This photo book is a tribute to the dedicated individuals, volunteers, artists, and spectators who have contributed to the magic of Zozobra over the decades. Through these stunning images, you will witness the evolution of this beloved event, from its humble origins to the grand centennial celebrations that mark a milestone in its history.

Join us as we revisit the joy, excitement, and spectacle of Zozobra through the lens of talented photographers who have captured the essence of this annual tradition. From the intricate details of Zozobra's construction to the vibrant energy of the crowds gathered to witness his fiery demise, each photograph tells a story of community, resilience, and the enduring power of ritual.

As you turn the pages of this book, may you feel the warmth of the flames, hear the echoes of laughter and cheers, and experience the magic that makes Zozobra a cherished part of Santa Fe's cultural tapestry. Let these images serve as a reminder of the bonds that unite us, the traditions that define us, and the spirit of Zozobra that lives on in all of us.

Thank you for joining us on this visual journey through a century of Zozobra. May these photographs ignite your imagination, spark your curiosity, and inspire you to embrace the magic of this beloved tradition for the next hundred years and beyond.

Ray Sandoval
Zozobra Event Chairman, August 2024

Photo Credits: This Page: Melinda Herrera. Opposite Page: Courtesy Palace of the Governors Photo Archives (NMHM/DCA), #HP.2014.14.1637.

4

Zozobra is not our martyr,
he is not our sacrifice.
He can only be defeated
by the continued goodwill
of the citizens of Santa Fe.
If they can't... summon
more goodwill than despair
each year... Zozobra triumphs.

- Will Shuster

Zozobra
100

CONTENTS

Introduction
A Burning Tradition:

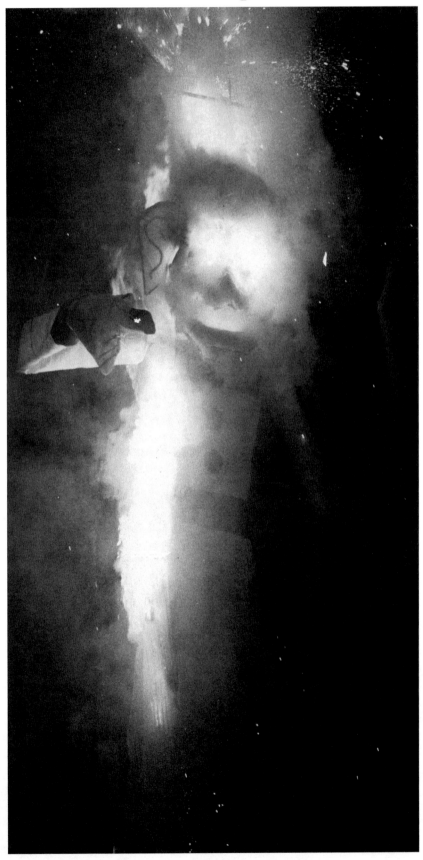

Photo Credits: This Page: Mark Lennihan, Courtesy Palace of the Governors Photo Archives (NMHM/DCA) #HP.2014.14.3032. Opposite Page: Bryce Risley.

Celebrating 100 Years of Zozobra in Santa Fe

Zozobra is a tradition, a touchstone, and a cultural treasure for the Santa Fe community, a unique phenomenon that helps define the Santa Fe identity. The annual burning of Old Man Gloom (aka "OMG" in this book) is both exhilarating and frightening (at least to little children), a spectacle to behold like no other. People of all ages watch in wide-eyed wonder as the 50-foot monster comes alive, then is teased, taunted, and burned under spectacular fireworks. He represents our woes and tribulations, and when he goes up in flames so too does our gloom. He offers us renewal, a chance to start over, and we gladly take it.

The Burning of Zozobra event is also a lot of fun. A big end-of-summer party in Santa Fe and the start of Fiestas. Meet your friends and family on the field, meet some strangers. Have some food, dance to the music, and best of all, yell "Burn Him!" a couple dozen times. Project your glooms onto the monster on the hill knowing that positivity will win over doom and gloom again this year. It's a powerful feeling.

How do you tell someone about Zozobra? It's difficult, words alone can't do it justice. We generally say: you have to be there in person and feel the energy, *you have to see it to believe it*. At least once, or maybe every year. A dramatic flaming pagan-ish ceremony in the City of Holy Faith? Check. A fun way to liven up a once-solemn community celebration? Check. A grand and meaningful expression of optimism through performance art for our historic, creative community? Definitely. All that and so much more.

The Zozobra Centennial is a good time to reflect on Zozobra's origins and his continuing life in our small town, to see how he got here, how he changed with the times, and how he continues to inspire the people of The City Different. This book celebrates those 100 years of Zozobra and the relationship of the Santa Fe community to this strange and wonderful event. We provide background and context for the birth, life, and death of the gloomy monster-marionette. We show how Old Man Gloom has been embraced and loved by Santa Fe over the years. We share the not-well-known meaning of the effigy-burning "Pageant of Gloom and Joy." We document the rise and fall -- and rise and fall again each year -- of our favorite boogeyman.

So don't forget next August or early September, as Summer begins its slide into Fall, to write down whatever sadness and gloom you may want to shed (or just *think them* real clearly) and send them to Old Man Gloom, who will surely come to Santa Fe again. *Burn Him!*

ZO
ZO
BRA

Born of imagination as the embodiment of our darkness,
Zozobra was embraced by the Santa Fe community with
hope and faith in our ability to cast off negativity and replace
it with light. We have faced these primal forces with revelry
and seriousness every year for a hundred years.

As Zozobra stands tall on a downtown hillside,
his legacy stands tall in our community identity.
As he burns bright in his dramatic death,
he also burns bright in our hearts.

Photo by Melinda Herrera.

100 YEARS

The mix of fun and fantasy and feelings of renewal have made Zozobra an irresistable force in our lives. He's been with us all these years through thick and thin, through good times and bad, and we can't imagine a time where Old Man Gloom doesn't come to town.

Here's looking at you, Zozobra, and to another 100 years of burning gloom!

Burning effigies

that symbolize
adverse forces in life
has been a part of annual rituals in
many cultures and traditions around
the world throughout history. While
some effigy-burning traditions utilize
the effigy-sculptures to represent
specific people (often political
or religious), other traditions
use effigies to represent more

conceptual and natural elements of life, like the change of seasons or the cycle of life-death-and-rebirth. Burning a representational effigy allows the participants to celebrate the symbolic defeat of those hardships and dark primal forces.

The need to defeat darkness

is strong in the human psyche, and that struggle has been told and retold in countless ways across the ages. Powerful and timeless stories are passed across generations; literature and movies are often built on this archetypal conflict (looking at you Darth Vader).

Human nature's inherent longing for the light drives the never-ending need to fight all forms of darkness, including our own. It's a profoundly satisfying experience to battle these symbols of darkness and overcome them.

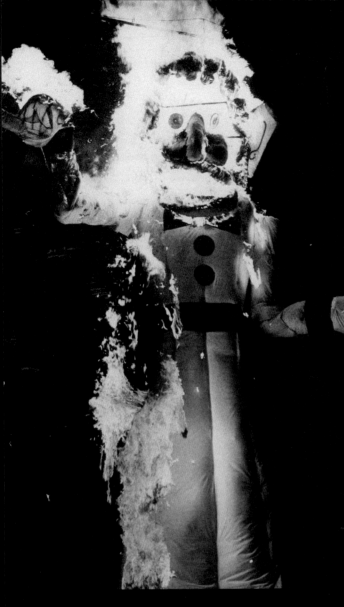

Fire is a
powerful and
mysterious element,
dangerous yet beneficial.
And what better way to battle
darkness than with fire? Fire is
transformational, turning physical
matter to energy and ash, to
smoke and heat. And to light.

Fire demands our attention, and we're hard-pressed to look away. Right in front of our eyes, as we watch the beautiful, dancing flames do their work, whatever is burning is suddenly… gone. Fire is the perfect way to eliminate representations of darkness and replace them with lightness, because fire, by its very nature, creates light.

represents the
dark feelings of
depression, sadness,
anxiety, and gloom.
We confront our
darkness-effigy, and using
the transformational
power of fire we burn
him up, banishing our
gloom. This act of defiance
and empowerment allows
the light feelings of
joy and happiness
back into our lives.

and we destroy him
and what he stands for.
Then we celebrate
the defeat of darkness
and the victory of light.

We call him
Zozobra.

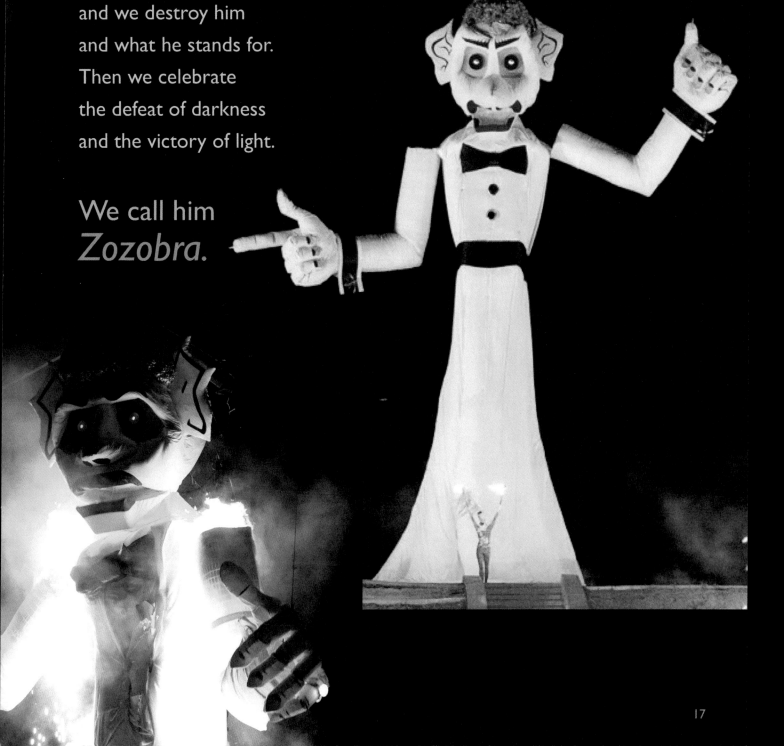

Section One:

Something strange and wonderful happened in Santa Fe in the 1920s. That something -- known as Zozobra -- grew larger and more powerful, and it continues to fascinate The City Different.

Beginnings

Evolution

ZOZOBRA

Battling Gloom

The Pageant 52

Every year Gloom and Joy fight it out on the hill in an epic battle for the ages.

The Players 58

A Fire Spirit, a gang of Gloomies, and the Santa Fe Community play important roles in defeating Old Man Gloom.

Building the Beast

Zozobradores 66

A devoted crew of volunteers build the giant gloom beast every year in a never-ending expression of love, passion, and fun.

The Gloomy Monster That

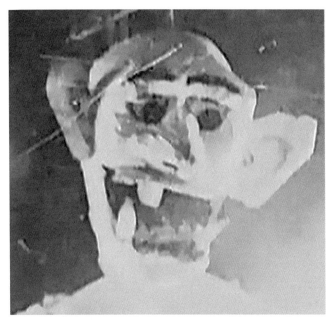

Old Man Gloom (OMG) was born in 1924 when artist Will Shuster built and burned the first effigy in Santa Fe which would come to be known as Zozobra. This was done at a backyard party hosted by Shuster and some of his artist friends. The group had complained that the annual Santa Fe Fiesta was too serious, too somber and not lively or fun enough. They pitched the idea to the official Fiesta Council that they might stage some fun events as part of Fiesta, but the Council denied this offer to liven up the centuries-old Fiesta event. So Shuster and his crew decided to stage their own private weekend Fiesta party, calling it "El Pasa Tiempo". They danced and paraded in festive costumes, and they burned a 6-foot tall effigy – a human-like "beast" symbolizing negativity.

They did it again in 1925, in another backyard party with a larger crowd and a 12-feet-tall monster. It was a rollicking good time.

As word of these feel-good, effigy-burning parties spread, Shuster was asked by City Officials to bring his fiery event to a downtown city lot for the entire community to witness on the first night of Fiesta in 1926. The Fiesta Council now agreed that it would be a spectacular start to the Fiesta weekend. Local newspaper editor E. Dana Johnson helped Shuster find an official name for the gloomy beast, and they

"Zozobra" means "anxiety, worry, gloom." The large effigy was called by various names in the early days, including:

- Old Man Groucher
- Old Man Depression
- Old Man Worry
- Old Man Gloom
- The Gloom King
- El Viejito Muy Malo
- The Fiesta Frankenstein
- The Gloom Beast
- The Boogeyman
- The Santa Fe Monster

Zozobra's lesser-known (and seldom seen) cousin is called "Tio Coco."

Charmed Santa Fe

settled on "Zozobra," found in the back of a Spanish dictionary, meaning "anguish, anxiety, gloom." Shuster and his friends built a 12-foot tall version of their gloom-monster (now simultaneously hideous and goofy) and packed him with colorful explosives. They staged a more elaborate ritual with dancing robed figures holding torches, who then dropped their robes and began dancing festively in bright party attire once the beast had burned. The audience of several hundred cheered, and all agreed that they felt a tremendous relief. The spirit of fun and celebration at the start of Fiesta was established as Zozobra was now fully born into the community of Santa Fe.

And so it came to be that Will Shuster was invited to bring his burning Gloom Monster to start Fiesta in Santa Fe every year thereafter. Zozobra grew taller, and in 1935 he was given a spot for his annual funeral pyre on a hillside in a new park just north of downtown with plenty of room for the community to bear witness and celebrate at his feet. Shuster rose to the occasion and built Santa Fe a terrific beast -- now also known as "Old Man Gloom." Zozobra grew taller (40-feet-tall in 1928) and more animated; he growled as his head turned and his arms moved, and the burning production-ceremony-ritual became more elaborate.

continued on next page

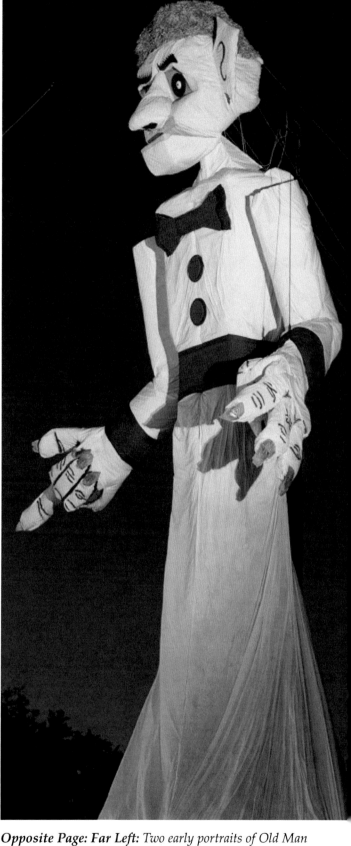

Opposite Page: Far Left: *Two early portraits of Old Man Gloom from the 1930s;* ***Center Left:*** *A middle-years mug shot in 1980.* ***This Page: Left:*** *Zozobra posing in full-color glory in the early 2000s.* ***Above:*** *Old Man Gloom defiantly surveys the crowd in 2013.*

Photo Credits: Opposite Page: Far Left Both Unknown, Public Domain. Center: Courtesy Palace of the Governors Photo Archives (NMHM/DCA), #HP.2014.14.1627. This Page: Left: Melinda Herrera. Above: Andres Maestas.

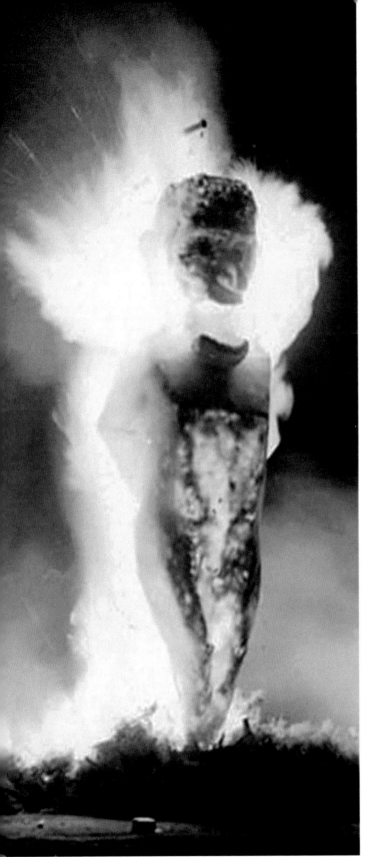

Zozobra's Primal

In 1939, a new-to-Santa Fe professional dancer, Jacques Cartier, was invited to create the powerful role of a dancing Fire Spirit that dramatically taunts then defeats Zozobra.

Crowds grew from several hundred to several thousand to tens of thousands as the Burning of Old Man Gloom became a must-see Santa Fe ritual kicking-off a worry-free Fiesta weekend, which now included a Children's Pet Parade and a Hysterical-Historical parade.

Shuster created a mythic backstory for Zozobra, and he encouraged people to put their woes and worries into the gloomy monster year after year. And people literally did so, stuffing Zozobra with all sorts of meaningful flammables: police reports, divorce papers, mortgages, written-down wishes, hopes and dreams. Shuster staged spectacular, fun-for-all ceremonies for decades, until he handed Old Man Gloom to the Kiwanis Club of Santa Fe in 1964. His friends in Kiwanis had been helping build and

This description of the first public burning of Zozobra appeared in the September 2, 1926, edition of the Santa Fe New Mexican:

Following vespers at the Cathedral, a long procession headed by the Conquistadores Band marched to the vacant space back of the City Hall, where Zozobra, a hideous effigy figure, 20 feet high, produced by the magic wand of Will Shuster, stood in ghastly silence, illuminated by weird, green fires. While the band played a funeral march, a group of

Kiwanians in black robes and hoods stole around the figure, with four others seated before the green fires.

When City Attorney, Jack Kennedy (on behalf of the absent Mayor), solemnly uttered the death sentence of Zozobra (with Isadoro Armijo as interpreter) and fired several revolver shots at the monster, the green fires changed to red, the surrounding ring of bonfires were ignited, red fires blazed at the foot of the figure, and a match was applied to its base, the fire leaping into a column of many colored flames.

Power Endures

stage the event from the very beginning, so it was a logical choice. The Fire Spirit role has also been turned over to younger dancers through the years, and the tradition continues.

Zozobra and the myth of Old Man Gloom have grown year in and year out. Santa Feans know well that they can project their gloom and negativity onto this crazy wood-and-cloth beast, and the world feels better once he – along with their gloom – is burned. They know this end-of-summer-start-of-Fiesta ritual will make everyone feel better, if even for a little while.

In 2024, Zozobra turned 100 years old, and the ritual of burning Old Man Gloom is firmly embedded in Santa Fe culture, like eating chile, red and green. It's something we do, it must be done. As Shuster noted, Zozobra "can only be defeated by the goodwill of the citizens of Santa Fe. If they cannot summon more goodwill then despair each year the Zozobra triumphs."

As it burned, and the encircling fires blazed brighter, there was a staccato of exploding fireworks from the figure and round about. Throwing off their black robes, the spectators emerged in gala costume, joining an invading army of bright-hued harlequins with torches in a dance around the fires, as the band struck up "La Cucaracha." The crowd then marched back between bonfires lining the streets to the armory and the big baile was on. It brought out the biggest crowd of native merrymakers seen here for years.

The fantastical image of a gigantic burning effigy and the primal power of fire to captivate one's gaze and imagination have drawn massive crowds to Santa Fe's annual Zozobra event since 1924. The effigy, also known as Old Man Gloom, is shown here in full burning glory in early-1930s (left) and 2019 (above). Santa Feans and visitors alike pack the field each year to participate in the event, chanting "Burn Him."

Photo Credits: Opposite Page, Top Left: Unknown, Public Domain. Center: Aaron Newsom;. This Page: Above: Melinda Herrera.

Zozobra and Fiesta: Balancing the Sacred

Above: *Members of the Fiesta Court representing de Vargas and his men survey Zozobra's crowd in 1986.* ***Opposite Page: Top Right:*** *Mariachis serenade the crowd, adding to the the festive mood under the watchful eyes of Zozobra in 2022.* ***Bottom Right:*** *The 2022 Fiesta Court celebrate Zozobra's defeat in front of his smoldering remains. Gloom is now gone and Fiestas de Santa Fe has begun.*

Fiesta de Santa Fe is an old ceremony -- perhaps one of the oldest in the United States – in an old city. The annual event was established in 1712 by proclamation specifying a mass, vespers and a sermon, serious religious components to commemorate and honor the resettlement of Santa Fe by Don Diego de Vargas in 1692 after 12 years of exile following the 1680 Pueblo Revolt.

Questions about the relationship of Zozobra to the Santa Fe Fiesta are natural, specifically: How did it come to be that a seemingly pagan ritual – the burning-at-the-stake of a 50-foot-tall hideous marionette-monster-effigy -- would be so associated with this solemn, Catholic Fiesta ceremony? How did the profane get mixed with the sacred in Santa Fe, The City of Holy Faith?

When Will Shuster and his friends suggested the idea of adding some "fun" events to liven up the 212th Fiestas in 1924, they were rebuffed by the Fiesta Council, its official organizers. Shuster and friends went ahead and staged their alternative fiesta *"El Pasa Tiempo"* as a private affair, and after two years the public sentiment was so strong for these festive celebrations – particularly for the effigy-burning part – that the Fiesta Council changed its mind and, with Santa Fe City officials, invited Shuster to stage his production for the public in the middle of town to start the 214th weekend Fiesta celebration in 1926. *(Why not... it's all good fun!)* Ever since, in the minds of most people, The Burning of Zozobra and the Santa Fe Fiesta have been linked.

When Old Man Gloom made his spectacular appearance (and fiery disappearance) every year over the decades since, he basically announced the commencement of Fiestas, although semi-officially and never under the direct guidance of the Fiesta Council (who probably were glad they didn't have to deal with that strange, enormous event). It was a loose alliance of the sacred and the

and the Profane

profane, a not-unreasonable balance of the human condition perhaps. The Fiesta Court briefly paraded at Zozobra's feet while Fiesta songs were sung and music played, then the gloom-monster was burned. A splendid time was guaranteed for all. Shuster must have been pleased to see his beastly event bring so much joy to the community as he intended.

Burn Him!

Viva la Fiesta!

Que Viva!

Alas, as the Zozobra event got more popular and the crowds grew larger, the logistics of staging that event on Friday night at the start of Fiesta proved too challenging. Crowds of 40-to-50-to-60-thousand spirited people flowing into the plaza after the burn could not be safely managed. So in the late 1990s "Burn Night" was moved away from Fiesta Friday, first to the Thursday prior, then to Friday night of the weekend before Fiesta (the Friday of Labor Day weekend). Further distanced from Fiesta weekend itself, Zozobra now stands tall with his own truly separate event, crazy as it is, in the City of Holy Faith, groaning in his fiery demise and still announcing to all that Fiesta is coming soon.

While the decidedly secular Burning of Old Man Gloom is technically "separate" from Fiesta, parts of Fiesta still find their way into the event, where you will briefly see the Fiesta Court and hear mariachis and shouted chants of "Viva la Fiesta!" Zozobra still remains the de facto start of Fiesta de Santa Fe in most peoples' minds, by association and by tradition. This balance is solidly embedded in the Santa Fe culture, this somewhat unholy alliance of a raucous boogeyman party with a prayerful historic celebration.

Other secular components of Santa Fe's Fiesta weekend which were initiated by Shuster and "The Cincos" and other friends in the mid-1920s include The Children's Pet Parade (Desfile de los Ninos) and the Hysterical/Historical Parade. They continue to this day as Fiesta events under the auspices of the Fiesta Council.

Santa Fe celebrated its 312th Fiestas in 2024 when Zozobra turned 100, so Old Man Gloom is new to the party!

Will Shuster: He Created

*Will Shuster was an out-going and friendly creative-spirit-about-town when he started Santa Fe's Zozobra tradition in 1924. He was a professional painter, one of Santa Fe's "Cinco Pintores" group of artists. **Above:** The proud creator poses with his enourmous grouchy monster, Old Man Gloom. **Opposite Page: Center Right:** Fun-loving Shuster enjoying Fiesta. **Top Right:** "Shus" is seen painting a mural on a courtyard wall in the NM Museum of Art in 1934.*

Photo Credits: Above: Courtesy Palace of the Governors Photo Archives (NMHM/DCA), #027852. Opposite Page: Center Right: Robert H. Martin, Courtesy Palace of the Governors Photo Archives (NMHM/DCA), #040201. Top Right: R.H. Dawson, Courtesy Palace of the Governors Photo Archives (NMHM/DCA), #030849.

William Howard "Will" Shuster Jr. was born in 1893 in Philadelphia, PA. He served in the US Army in France during World War I, where he suffered from German gas attacks. After the war, his doctor recommended that he go to the mountain West where his injured lungs might heal in the dry thin air. A budding painter, Shuster and his wife came to Santa Fe in Spring 1920 where he settled in and befriended several other up-and-coming artists. This group of five painters became known around town as "Los Cinco Pintores" (or just "The Cincos"). They made an impression on the community and helped stimulate the burgeoning Santa Fe art scene of the early 1920s.

Shuster, or just "Shus" to most folks, was a friendly and gregarious person, quick to smile and laugh and befriend everyone he met. His positive outlook on life would be amplified and forever represented by his greatest artistic achievement: the annual public performance for the Santa Fe community in which a human-sized Fire Spirit battles the giant gloom-monster Zozobra.

One anecdote provides an example of how Shus thought, which perhaps became the seed of an idea for The Burning of Old Man Gloom. On a cold Winter evening in January 1924, Shus and his friends were gathered around a table in the La Fonda bar. Shus had just sold a painting, so he was happy and buying the drinks. But his fellow Cincos were gloomy, thinking about their lot as "starving artists" and not so excited by Shus' good fortune. To cheer up his crew, Shus suggested they write down their complaints on paper, then he placed them in an ashtray on the table and lit them on fire. The bartender was not amused, as you might imagine, and The Cincos were quickly kicked out of La Fonda.

A few months later, in the Spring of 1924, Shus heard stories from friends about Easter Holy Week traditions in the Yaqui Indian

a Monster

communities of Arizona and Mexico, in which an effigy of Judas was paraded around the village and ultimately set alight. Shus claimed that this idea formed the basis of his Burning of Zozobra performance. (Of course, burning effigies -- whether representing "concepts" or real people – has been done across millennia by cultures worldwide. Something about the transformational power of fire.)

By the time Summer 1924 was underway, Shus and The Cincos and their friends had decided that the upcoming Fiesta de Santa Fe needed some livening up, as they complained that the highly-religious Fiesta events were too morose, too serious. They envisioned multiple events during the Fiesta weekend that would create some gaiety and brighten everyone's spirits. They pitched this idea to the Fiesta Council, but it was turned down. The Council, of course, was focused on continuing a

continued on next page

Shuster's first gloom effigy in 1924 had a tiny undersized head due to a miscommunication between Shuster and his friend Gustave Baumann, who made the head. (Bauman is a famed Santa Fe artist, printmaker, and puppet-maker.) Shus later laughed about it and called it a "pin head," and he personally built Zozobra's head every year after that.

Shuster recalled a time in the early 1930s when they were ready to start the burn and he realized he hadn't brought any matches to light the fuse. A Boy Scout working on the production was dispatched into the crowd, and he successfully procured matches to start the show.

During World War II Shuster found it difficult to find the materials he needed to build his gloom monster, and there was a shortage of men to help build and stage the event. In 1944 a miniature effigy was built and then burned on the NW corner of the Plaza. It disappointed everyone.

In 1946, the burn was cancelled due to drought (fire danger) and lack of materials. Several of Shus' friends were so disappointed that they snuck over to Ft. Marcy Park and attempted to burn the "Zozobra Pole." The inebriated men later reported it as a less-than-satisfying experience.

In the late 1940s, the Mexican Consulate was scheduled to speak on stage during the burning event. As his group made their way to the microphone, one of the Gloomies inadvertently lit the fuse to Zozobra, and the group of diplomats narrowly escaped the flames.

The Artist Became

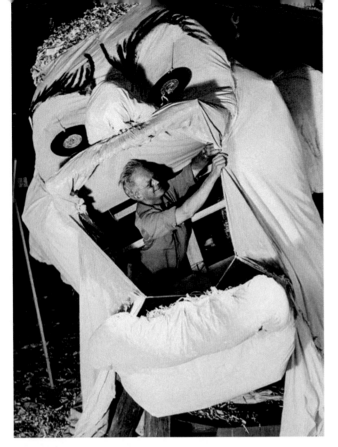

212-year tradition of solemnly honoring the hardships of the Spanish founders of Santa Fe.

Not ones to be denied, the creative Santa Fe newcomers decided that they would stage their own alternative Fiesta celebration. They dubbed this private weekend-long party "El Pasa Tiempo," with much music and dancing. The highlight of these backyard festivities was the burning of Shuster's 6-foot effigy, made of wood, wire and cotton cloth. He was an eerie character, nameless in 1924, part ghost and part monster. It was a hit, and they did it again in 1925.

Word of the fun festivities, and especially the astonishing burning of the gloom-monster spread in the community, and Shus was asked to bring his event – and his monster – for a public burning behind City Hall in 1926. The Fiesta Council agreed this time that Santa Fe's annual Fiesta celebration could make room for some fun amid the prayers. Working with a friend, Shuster found a name for his gloom-monster: "Zozobra" (meaning depression, anxiety,

ZOZOBRA

Will Shuster gladly carried the burden of building the giant effigy and staging the spectacular production for the Santa Fe community every year for 40 years. He had help of course, including the "20-30 Club," local Boy Scouts, many of his artist friends, and his friends in the SF Kiwanis Club. **Above top:** Shus adjusts the fabric skin around the mouth of the massive marionette. **Above:** Zozobra was such a beloved phenomenon throughout New Mexico that Shus was asked to design a Fiesta-themed float to represent the state in the 1950 Rose Parade in Pasadena, California. The float featured Indian dancers and members of the Santa Fe Fiesta Court, framed by a large Zia Sun in back and a friendly Old Man Gloom in front. It won the First Place "National Trophy" award for out-of-state floats. **Opposite Page: Center:** Shuster showing off Zozobra's shredded-paper guts. **Far Right:** Shuster touching his monstrous creation as fireworks and other flammable materials are loaded into Zozobra's backside.

Shuster's early Zozobras were simple figures tied to a pole. They later became more sophisticated marionettes with moveable (animated) arms, head and jaw.

In 2001, Zozobra was recognized by the Guiness Book of World Records as the "Largest Marionette in the World."

Despite reports in the press, Zozobra has never been made of "paper mache." He has always been constructed with cloth over a wood-and-wire frame.

Dancer Jacques Cartier was not involved in the original creation of Zozobra in the mid-1920s. In 1939, Shuster asked him to create and perform a spectacular dance for the event, and Cartier created the role of the "Fire Spirit" as part of the "Pageant of Gloom and Joy." He danced that role for 30 years.

As a professional visual artist (painter), Will Shuster saw the staging of the Burning of Zozobra as a way to "paint the night sky" on a large scale using fire, smoke and fireworks. He was successful!

a Gloom Buster

gloom in Spanish), and they built a larger, 12-foot-tall effigy stuffed with colorful explosives. Mounds of dry tumbleweeds were piled at his feet. This first "public" burning was very successful, and Shus was the toast of the town. He was invited back annually, and in 1935 the City provided a special location for burning Zozobra on a hillside next to a new park (also the High School "stadium"). The burning production grew more sophisticated, and the gloom-monster grew taller and more animated, as did the crowds. Santa Fe loved Zozobra, their Old Man Gloom.

Shuster carried the burden of the event and personally oversaw the construction of the massive marionette for decades until 1964. Year in and year out, Shus and his friends scrounged materials and spent a full month building Zozobra and preparing for the burn. It was a huge commitment, but Shus did it without complaint, for he understood the

continued on next page

Photo Credits: Opposite Page: Top Left: Unkown. Public Doimain. Lower Left: Courtesy Palace of the Governors Photo Archives (NMHM/DCA), #049923. This Page: Left: Courtesy Palace of the Governors Photo Archives (NMHM/DCA), #030476. Above: Henry Dendahl, Courtesy Palace of the Governors Photo Archives (NMHM/DCA), #057751.

Shuster's Legacy is Santa Fe History

importance of casting off one's gloom, the importance to the Santa Fe Community. In 1964, the aging artist gave the legal rights (and responsibility) -- along with his detailed model and archive of drawings and scripts -- to the Kiwanis Club of Santa Fe. Shus wanted to ensure the successful continuation of this beloved, historic tradition, and Kiwanis was committed to do so.

Shuster died five years later, on Feb. 9, 1969. We imagine he died a happy man, knowing with a characteristic glint in his eye how much joy he provided to his beloved Santa Fe over the years, and knowing that his artistic legacy lives on, allowing tens of thousands of people to release their worries every year, burning their gloom into the future, forevermore.

Thank you Shus!

This Page: Top Left: Shus (bottom row in white shirt) and his "Zozobradores" pose at OMG's feet in 1953. Left: A dapper Will Shuster strolls the Santa Fe Plaza in style during Fiesta, ca. 1950. Opposite Page: Top: Shus shows off his giant marrionette to some local kids, ca. 1960. Far Right: Shus and helpers catch their breath beside the massive head before it is hoisted into place. Near Right: An original Shuster family Christmas Card with Zozobra imagery, ca. 1943.

May bright canticles of
Peace + Joy + Love
Pervade this day
And those to come
For you + yours

A Monster of Many Faces

From Old Man Gloom's Historic Scrapbook: These early-years photographs of Zozobra show an evolution of faces and styles for Santa Fe's Gloom Monster. **This Page,** *clockwise starting top left: 1928, 1938, 1955, 1933.* **Opposite Page,** *clockwise starting top left: 1942, 1949, 1963, 1947, 1939.*

Photo Credits: All Unknown, Public Domain.

33

The 1920s & 1930s:

Old Man Gloom ("OMG" in this book) was born old in 1924, and he literally grew up in the 1920s and 1930s, from 6 to 12 feet to 20, then 40 feet tall. He moved around town from a private backyard to a public downtown lot to a hillside community ball field. In those early days he was sometimes called Old Man Groucher, Old Man Worry, the Gloom King, and *El Viejito Muy Malo*. He was a shape-shifting hideous monster with a floppy cigar, missing teeth, pointy ears, sometimes bald and sometimes bushy, but always mean and growling and very scary to the local kids.

Two of the earliest known photographs of Santa Fe's "Gloom King" show him in a downtown lot behind City Hall (now a library) in 1928 (above) and 1933 (right). He was burned in this lot from 1926 through 1935. Changing facial features show that Zozobra's image was dynamic in those early years, although his white cloak and cummerbund were always present.

When Old Man Gloom was Young

These early-years Zozobras are being prepped for the burning ceremony in 1936 (top left), 1937 (left), and 1938 (above), now stylin' with buttons. In 1936 the annual Zozobra event moved to Santa Fe's new city park next to the high school athletic field (Magers' Field), where cars parked on the field and walk-in pedestrians were not allowed. Huge piles of tumbleweeds were gathered from around town and piled at his feet, perfect pyres for burning the towering, gloomy "Fiesta Frankenstein."

The 1940s & 1950s:

The Burning of Zozobra was a well-established community event entering the 1940s, a wildly popular ritual marking the start of Fiesta. Despite a few set-backs in the mid-1940s due to the war -- a lack of materials and labor resulted in smaller effigies in 1944 and 1945 -- Zozobra returned for his annual celebration stronger than ever moving into the 1950s. The ballpark would fill with thousands of people in hundreds of cars (and no walk-ins allowed!) to celebrate the end of gloom with a festive drive-in-movie atmosphere. Zozobra was now 40 feet tall, and his physical features became more consistent, establishing his look for decades to come.

Top Left: *A balding, dapper Zozobra poses with an admirer in 1940.* **Left:** *The 1943 effigy was a caricature-fusion of the three dictators the world was at war with, and named "Hiro-Hitle-Mus." This was the only Zozobra created to resemble or reference a real person. Shuster later said he regretted designing this effigy, claiming that an unknown, unrecognizable figure is more mysterious and more powerful.* **Above:** *A classic Old Man Gloom awaits his fiery destiny upon a pile of oil-soaked tumbleweeds, ca. 1949.*

Zozobra Comes of Age

Above Left: The giant grouchy beast is hung onto his burn pole in 1959. That year's version sported fancy matching belt and cuffs and was the second appearance of a tie (the first was in 1956). Many features of Zozobra's classic, trademark "look" took hold in the 1950s. *Above:* The 1955 Zozobra is shown in the mood for Fiesta, posing with a Fiesta belle. *Left:* The 1950 Gloom King in a rare color photograph from that era.

The 1960s & 1970s:

Old Man Gloom faithfully returned each year to take his place on the hill overlooking the Ft. Marcy ballfield and scare/entertain new generations of Santa Feans. In the 1960s and 1970s, his image was set; his tie, cuffs, hair, eyes and lips changed little as he was now locked in our collective imaginations. But other changes occured: Creator Will Shuster gave the rights and responsibilities for Zozobra to the Santa Fe Kiwanis Club in 1964, and in 1975 cars were banned from the field, displeasing many folks but making it a pedestrian-friendly event.

*Above: An agitated Zozobra waves his arms as he reacts to taunts by the Fire Spirit in 1968. **Top right:** The 1960 gloom monster surveys the scene from his hillside perch on a sunny afternoon. **Right:** Old Man Gloom fights another losing battle for his life in 1961.*

The Giant Gloom Monster Hits His Stride

*The popularity of the annual gloom-busting ceremony sky-rocketed during these decades, with tens of thousands attending each burn, even as modest admission prices were now charged for the formerly free event. Classic "70s style" Zozobras are seen here in 1971 (**left**) flashing a peace sign to the Fire Spirit (a trick perhaps?); 1976 at sunset (**below left**); and in 1978 (**below**) giving a traditional pre-burn "thumbs-up."*

Photo Credits: This Page: Above: Tony O'Brien, Courtesy Palace of the Governors Photo Archives (NMHM/DCA), #HP.2014.14.1638. All Other Photos: Unknown, Public Domain.

The 1980s & 1990s:

Zozobra now stands menacingly at 50 feet tall at the close of the 20th century, and massive crowds attend to witness the end of their collective gloom for another year. Raucous chants of "Burn Him! Burn Him!" come from young and old alike, encouraging the Fire Spirit to terminate the miserable monster again. All are awed and wide-eyed at the modern pagan spectacle. 1984 saw the first ever TV broadcast of the burning, but that didn't keep crowds down, even as the price of admission rose from $1 to $2 then $3 during the 1990s.

Above: Old Man Gloom stands bound against the afternoon breeze in 1986 as children watch in amazement. *Right:* The Fire Spirit confronts Zozobra in 1983.

Zozobra in His Prime

Zozobra remained ever-defiant in the light of day and dark of night throughout the 1990s, standing tall for anxiety, depression, melancholy and grouchiness, and always ready to confront his tormenters. **Top Left:** *Ready for his night of fame in 1998.* **Left:** *Battling Fire Spirits in 1994.* **Above:** *A spooky specter not quite hiding in the darkness in 1999.*

Photo Credits: Opposite Page, Far Left: Leslie Tallant, Courtesy Palace of the Governors Photo Archives (NMHM/DCA), #HP.2014.14.1632. All other photos: Unknown, Public Domain.

The 2000s & 2010s: *Old Man*

Old Man Gloom had finer features and seemed leaner and meaner in his old age in the early 21st century. The burning shows grew bigger and more spectacular, with more music, more dancers, more fireworks. The crowds grew larger too, testing the limits of the park. Although new security protocols were initiated after 9/11, people still came *en masse* to celebrate the end of negativity. In 2014 the "Decades Project" began as a lead-up to Zozobra's 100th birthday. These 10 years featured changing faces, bodies, clothing, and music that reflected the Gloom King's past.

Left, top to bottom: Zozobra came back in fine form in the 2000s to meet his fiery fate in The City Diffferent, 2002, 2006, 2007. **Above:** *A "classic" Old Man Gloom surveys the boistrous crowd and prepares for battle in 2013 prior to the Decades Project.*

Gloom's Monster Memories

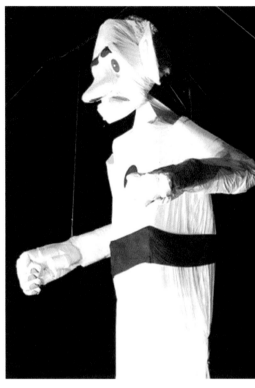

The Zozobra "Decades Project" was an homage to a long life (and quick death) through changing times and styles with modern interpretations or re-creations of various stages of Zozobra's history. **Above Left:** 2014 - the 1920s, with a mustache and bare chest. **Above:** 2015 - the 1930s, bald and basic. **Left:** 2016 - the 1940s with a fedora and necktie. **Below:** 2017 - the 1950s with a cardigan sweater.

The 2010s & 2020s:

Zozobra dressed in a variety of styles as the Decades Project continued, with pop culture touchstones from each decade influencing the gloomy beast's presentation and show. Crowd sizes and ticket prices continued to grow as the shows became more sophisticated; security and crowd control also grew more complex and costly, a sign of the times. Despite a pause in 2020 for the pandemic lockdown (where a classic Zozobra returned for a televised-no-crowd event, the only live event in NM during the lockdown), the Decades Project finished in 2023 in magical style.

The "Decades Project" continues. **Above:** *2018 - the 1960s are represented with bolo and belt.* **Below:** *2019 - the 1970s are noted in disco style and Zozobra's hoping he's "staying alive."* **Right:** *2020 saw a pause in the Decades Project due to the pandemic, with a retro-classic Zozobra. It was "back to basics," and he burned with no crowd.*

Recreating Zozobra's Gloomy Decades

The "Decades Project" concludes. **Top left:** *2021 - the 1980s are noted in a ghoulish "Thriller" style with green makeup and red leather jacket.* **Left:** *2022 - the 1990s are shown with suspenders and arm tats.* **Above:** *2023 - the 2000s are represented in full wizard style with wand and cape. But no magic spell could save this beast!*

Photo Credits: Opposite Page: All photos by Melinda Herrera.
This Page: All photos by Bryce Risley.

100 Years Old in 2024:

100 years of Zozobra is a major milestone for the Santa Fe community, and the 2024 Burning of Old Man Gloom was a spectacular celebration. Zozobra himself was dressed up smartly (and appropriately) for the occassion; a Centennial Torch relay brought fire across town to OMG's feet; a special drone show wowed the sold-out crowd; and a better-than-ever fireworks show capped off the evening. No one was disappointed, and surely no one will forget this night!

Some suggest that Zozobra "started" in 1926 when he first appeared in public in a city lot. But it's clear that Old Man Gloom was first created and burned in 1924 in a private backyard party, so it's fitting that Zozobra's 100th birthday was celebrated in 2024.

The Santa Fe community looks forward to another 100 years of burning Zozobra and banishing our gloom.

Photo Credits: This Page: Above: Melinda Herrera. Right: Bryce Risley. Opposite Page: Center Top: Bryce Risley. Center Bottom: Daniel Clavio. Far Right: Melinda Herrera.

A Happy Birthday Burning Bash for Zozobra

Opposite Page: Far Left: *The 2024 Centennial Zozobra -- Old Man Gloom #100 -- looks dapper in a white tuxedo as he groans in protest of the Fire Spirit doing battle at his feet.* ***Center:*** *Golden-haired Zozobra stands tall as Fiesta dancers entertain the crowd.* ***This Page: Left (2):*** *A Centennial drone show flew in the night sky above OMG, dazzling the crowd. The robotic flying lights created emojis and words above Zozobra before and during the fireworks show.* ***Above:*** *Zozobra burns in the finale of this truly special 100th Anniversary event for a record Santa Fe crowd.*

Zozobra's

The Zozobra Centennial (100th Anniversary / Birthday) was celebrated throughout the year leading up to the 100th burn on August 30, 2024. Special events included a fabulous Gala 100th Birthday Bash in April, the imaginative "Painted Zozobra Sculptures" art project in June, three splendid new Zozobra-related shows at New Mexico Museums (History, Art, and Folk Art), an insightful documentary film ("*Zozobra: 100 Years of Fire and Redemption*"), a whimsical and touching original opera production at the Lensic, and the premier of the new awe-inspiring Zozobra-shaped hot air balloon. Other Centennial commemorations included the official re-naming of the City's historical burn event park ("Zozobra Field at Fort Marcy Park") with a new sign with Zozobra time capsules placed beneath, plus the permanent installation of a large sculpture of Zozobra behind the Santa Fe Convention Center.

Above: An enormous 135' tall Zozobra-shaped hot air balloon named was created for the Centennial with support from the Cities of Santa Fe and Albuquerque. It was premiered in Santa Fe at the 100th burn on August 30th, 2024, and it delighted fans again at the 2024 Albuquerque Balloon Fiesta in October. This extra-large balloon dwarfs the giant effigy himself. Right: A 21' tall steel sculpture of Zozobra by Don Kennell was installed at the Convention Center in August 2024 to commemorate Zozobra's 100th year.

Centennial Commemorated in SF Style

This lyric from *"Zozobra: The Revenge"* captures the essence of The Burning of Zozobra:

*Let's start
right now
Seeing the best
in each other,
Start right now
Seeing the best
in ourselves.
We can do
this together,
Set our
fire alight,
Together we
can burn
our despair,
And laugh
at the night!*

Lyric by Joe Illick.

Above: The theatrical production entitled "Zozobra: The Revenge" was staged at the Lensic in Santa Fe during the weekend of the Centennial burn. The opera, composed by Joe Illick and written by Doug Preston, featured Zozobra's epic battle with the Fire Spirit and the release of his Gloomie minions.

Below: The 2024 "Painted Zozobra Sculptures" project saw 33 artists reimagine and decorate 4' tall mini-Zozobras in a myriad of artistic styles. The sculptures were exhibited around town prior to being auctioned as a Zozobra fundraiser. The project was developed in partnership with the SF Gallery Association.

Celebrating Santa Fe's 100-Year-Old Monster

*Left: A special torch was created for Zozobra's Centennial and was run relay-style through Santa Fe on August 30, 2024 (the day of the 100th burn), from the Railyard to Fort Marcy Park and up onto the hill below OMG to light a symbolic Zia Sun, from which the Fire Spirit would later light her torches. Current Fire Spirit Helene Luna (in red) is shown here passing the torch to her replacement (starting in 2027), Than Povi Martinez. **Above:** The Museum of New Mexico helped celebrate Zozobra's Centennial by staging three commemorative shows, this one at the History Museum entitled "Zozobra: A Fire That Never Goes Out."*

Zozobra & Community Service

Kiwanis Connects Community Through Zozobra - the Joykiller!

for the Zozobra Centennial Gala

Buenas tardes! I'm Congresswoman Teresa Leger Fernandez, representing the beautiful and beautifully diverse third congressional district of New Mexico. I'm standing here just filled with gratitude, gratitude to be invited to join Kiwanis as you celebrate 100 years of the burning of Zozobra! Gratitude, because we are not just celebrating 100 years of burning our gloom away, but also almost 100 years of Kiwanis Connecting Community, of Kiwanis Creating Community by not just keeping this tradition alive, but by making it ever bigger, ever better, year after year.

So let's start with some Gritos, *Que Viva Kiwanis, Que Viva Las Fiestas, y Que Quema Zozobra, Siempre.* Thank you to the Kiwanis Club of Santa Fe for a century of delight and for letting me come here to shout Gratitude and Gritos with you.

Zozobra strikes at our most primal instincts. Children and adults alike need to scream. We need to release the negative to make space for the positive. It's a form of therapy, of liberation, and of catharsis ... But Zozobra manages to give us the space to scream and let go of what we don't want while still making us feel connected at the most fundamental

level. We are connected, not just because we are screaming at the top of our lungs with 60,000 thousand other people. We are connected because the event is at its core, an act of love. I always say that service is an act of love.

So I am suggesting that the thousands of volunteers who show up to give their most precious resource, time, to the building and burning of Zozobra, love the ritual, love the tradition, and but most importantly they love our community and each and every person who makes up that community and shows up to scream. You do it for the love of those who, like my father when he got too old, watched it on TV. And may I say, Ray Sandoval, your love appears infinitely expandable as you dedicate your incredible talent and operational organization to this community.

It's this connection, the one we make with each other, that carries us through the hardest times. In fact, connection is the foundation of every thriving community. In anticipation of the 100th, I listened to the interview of Will Shuster in the Smithsonian archives. A man who came here to die because of the Tuberculosis he contracted when he was gassed during WWI, ended up bequeathing our City so much. His creativity was unleashed as he formed friendships with other like-minded young artists, with the Fiesta Council, the editor of the New Mexican and as he noted, the Kiwanians

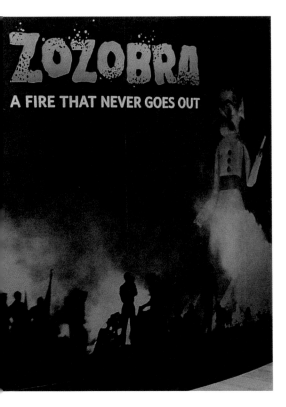

ZOZOBRA
A FIRE THAT NEVER GOES OUT

Right: A Once-in-a-Hundred-Years Gala celebration was held at La Fonda in April 2024 to commemorate the Zozobra Centennial. Top Right: Gala-goers raise their glasses to toast Zozobra's 100th Anniversay before they sing Happy Birthday to Old Man Gloom. The festive Gala, which featured an auction and a very special performance by the Fire Spirit, was a fundraiser for The Preservation of the Burning of Zozobra fund to support this traditional community event.

Photo Credits: Both Pages: Center: Daniel Clavio. All others by Bryce Risley.

who were the original gloomies. He paints murals for the WPA during the depression, that art project which gave us so much public art that still inspires today. Indeed, it inspired my own Creative Economy Revitalization Act.

In the archives of those early Zozobras, the front page of the newspaper has on its left, the headline: "Hitler ponders his next move", and on the right side the headline: "Fiesta Guests Prepare to Burn Zozobra, Top Joy Killer, at Stake Tonight." What a juxtaposition. I am reminded that in those dark days where Hitler had overturned German democracy and was preparing to wage a second world war, Zozobra helped Santa Fe buck the gloom.

But today, we too are at a precarious moment. We are at a time in American history, not the first time, but a time where people are questioning our ability to care for each other, our ability to see ourselves as part of something greater than our own self interests. We don't know if as a Nation we can see ourselves as Nosotros, and not Otros.

There are those who lament the decline of civility and rightfully worry about the future of our Democracy. But what I see here in Zozobra's legacy with the work of Kiwanis, the Fiesta Council, the Rotarians and so many more civic organizations in our town, is that Santa Feans are bucking that decline. The creativity that has fueled Santa Fe since before

Will Shuster arrived, and continues to stitch us together, helps us see others more fully. We celebrate the different, we are curious about each other and we carry on unique and different traditions - including Zozobra, Spanish Market, Indian Market, tribal feast days, and the Camino al Santuario. All events that are about learning about people who might not speak our language or share the same faith. We use art to connect, reflect and explore .

When you unveil the latest artistic version of Zozobra, you also unveil once again, a commitment to love and to community. You recommit Zozobra to service. You commit Zozobra to goodness. You, Kiwanis, working through the joy-killer Zozobra, are the antidote we need here and everywhere in our country to the malaise of isolation and fear that threatens to tear us apart.

As you stitch up a Zozo filled with divorce papers and sad news, you also stitch us together in joy and delight. By continuing to celebrate Zozobra and the traditions that keep Santa Fe's hearty alma alive, we continue to nurture a sense of unity, connection, and collective healing within our beautiful and diverse communities - and we do it together.

So let's end where we started, *Que Viva Kiwanis, Que Viva Las Fiestas, Y Que Viva Zozobra. Muchisimas gracias.*

Congresswoman Teresa Leger Fernandez, *April 2024*

Zozobra's Story: *Goodwill*

Zozobra is the nemesis of all that is good, and Santa Fe knows only too well the spell of darkness and despair that Zozobra casts annually over our City—our world.

This doom-and-gloom specter is reincarnated annually because of our own misdeeds, doubts, despair and depression that we as humans create throughout the year—"our collective gloom". The negative energy from all this gloom accumulates and combines to conjure the specter of gloom—ZOZOBRA. As more and more strange sightings and events occur, the city's governing officials decide they must act. In order to lure Zozobra out of hiding, the city leaders invite him to a party to be held in "his honor". With his enormous ego urging him on, Zozobra accepts this invitation, recognizing it as his best opportunity to invade the heart of town (his trojan horse), destroy all hope and happiness, and rob the city of its most precious possession, its hope.

Zozobra appears at Fort Marcy Park, just north of Santa Fe's heart — the Plaza — at the appointed hour dressed in his black-tie attire. Eager to set his sinister plans in motion, Zozobra becomes disgruntled as the merriment ensues. Once the sun disappears behind the mountains he seizes his opportunity, using his dark magic to thrust the town into darkness. In furtherance of his ominous plan, Zozobra casts a spell over Santa Fe's children, driving hope and happiness from their minds and replacing it with gloom and despair transforming them into his underlings, the Gloomies. Zozobra realizes the citizens have lured him to this fraudulent party to capture him, and he commands his now-faithful army of Gloomies to wreak havoc on the city. The Gloomies begin to enact his wicked plan, but a group of brave, torch-bearing townsfolk arrives to challenge Zozobra. Having no tools to fight him, they light their torches and challenge Zozobra with Fire! The childish ghouls, seeing the light from the lit torches wake as if from a nightmare. The children, roused back to their previous selves scatter and run back to their distraught parents.

This display of arrogance and the loss of his minions only infuriates Zozobra. Growling in vehemence, Zozobra chases the torchbearers away. Now there is nothing to stand in the way

Defeats Gloom and Doom

These original typed notes by Will Shuster explain the concept and stages of the Burning of Zozobra event, representing "the eternal struggle between darkness and light." *Courtesy of the Shuster Family.*

of Zozobra's takeover of the town. There is no one or nothing to stop him....but the crowd begins the age-old cry, "Burn him!"

As more and more people join in the chat, the citizens of Santa Fe feel the hope welling up from inside themselves. And just as our feelings of despair and gloom created Zozobra, our feeling of hope and caring for one another start to exude positive energy and goodwill into the darkness. Suddenly that good energy materializes into Zozobra's antithesis—the Fire Spirit. The Fire Spirit emerges from the collective hopes, dreams, and faith of Santa Fe's citizens. Asking the people of Santa Fe to invigorate his powers, the Fire Spirt commits to this eternal battle between good and evil. The Fire Spirit battles the darkness to bring forth light and vanquish Santa Fe's oldest foe. The Fire Spirit now dances with flaming torches, tormenting Zozobra, who shakes his arms in rage, glaring balefully down at his enemy. The crowd's fervent desire to see the monster defeated is realized as the Fire Spirit taunts Zozobra by using his powers to surround Zozobra with fireworks, adding insult to injury. The Fire Spirit ignites the air on both sides of Zozobra in a waterfall of fire that rains down from above. The crowd's hope to destroy Zozobra is now realized and further adds to the overwhelming power the Fire Spirt now has to conduct the battle. The Fire Spirt sets Zozobra alight in a towering blaze of fire and smoke.

Under a sky lit by celebratory fireworks, the flames consume Zozobra, and he collapses at last into a smoking pile of embers. The crowd dances joyfully as happiness and hope return to the city and state of Santa Fe, New Mexico. Having vanquished gloom for yet another year, the Fire Spirit disappears into the starry night. But alas, gloom will rise again out of man's failings, faults, and failures to accumulate in the next year's Zozobra. Once again, the Fire Spirit must be summoned to overcome gloom in an ageless dance that mirrors the eternal struggle between darkness and light. NOTE: Zozobra is not our martyr, he is not our sacrifice. He can only be defeated by the continued goodwill of the citizen of Santa Fe. If they cant not summon more goodwill then despair each year the Zozobra triumphs...

-Will "Shus" Shuster

'The Pageant of Gloom and Joy'

In 1939, Will Shuster and Jacques Cartier created the classic and familiar Zozobra performance that has endured over the decades -- entitled "The Pageant of Gloom and Joy" -- which is explained in Shus' own words (see previous pages).

Act 1: Zozobra Arrives

"In order to lure Zozobra out of hiding, the city's governing officials invite him to a party to be held in "his honor." With his enormous ego urging him on, Zozobra accepts this invitation, recognizing it as his best opportunity to invade the heart of town (his Trojan horse), destroy all hope and happiness, and rob the city of its most precious possession, its hope....

"Zozobra appears at Fort Marcy Park, just north of Santa Fe's heart – the Plaza – at the appointed hour dressed in his black-tie attire."

Photo Credits: This Page: Above: Tony O'Brien, Courtesy Palace of the Governors Photo Archives (NMHM/DCA), #HP.2014.14.1638. Opposite Page: Top Right: Unknown, Public Domain. Lower Right: Melinda Herrera.

– a Tragedy in Five Acts

Act 2: Gloomies Gather

"Once the sun disappears behind the mountains he seizes his opportunity, using his dark magic to thrust the town into darkness. In furtherance of his ominous plan, Zozobra casts a spell over Santa Fe's children, driving hope and happiness from their minds and replacing it with gloom and despair transforming them into his underlings, the Gloomies....

"Zozobra realizes the citizens have lured him to this fraudulent party to capture him, and he commands his now-faithful army of Gloomies to wreak havoc on the city."

"The Gloomies begin to enact his wicked plan, but a group of brave, torch-bearing townsfolk arrives to challenge Zozobra. Having no tools to fight him, they light their torches and challenge Zozobra with Fire! The childish ghouls, seeing light from the lit torches wake as if from a nightmare. The children, roused back to their previous selves scatter and run back to their distraught parents....

"This display of arrogance and the loss of his minions only infuriates Zozobra. Growling in vehemence, Zozobra chases the torchbearers away."

Act 3: Torch Bearers Resist

Hope and Positivity Prevail

Act 4: The Crowd Chants

"There is no one or nothing to stop him… but the crowd begins the age-old cry, "Burn him!"…

"And just as our feelings of despair and gloom created Zozobra, our feeling of hope and caring for one another start to exude positive energy and goodwill into the darkness. Suddenly that good energy materializes into Zozobra's antithesis – the Fire Spirit."

Photo Credits: This Page: Sydney Brink, Courtesy Palace of the Governors Photo Archives (NMHM/DCA), #HP.2014.14.1939. Opposite Page: Melinda Herrera.

Over Despair and Gloom

Act 5: The Fire Spirit Conquers

'The Fire Spirit emerges from the collective hopes, dreams, and faith of Santa Fe's citizens. Asking the people of Santa Fe to invigorate his powers, the Fire Spirit commits to this eternal battle between good and evil....

"The Fire Spirit battles the darkness to bring forth light and vanquish Santa Fe's oldest foe....

"The crowd's hope to destroy Zozobra is now realized and further adds to the overwhelming power the Fire Spirit now has to conduct the battle. The Fire Spirit sets Zozobra alight in a towering blaze of fire and smoke....

"The crowd dances joyfully as happiness and hope return."

The Main Event: Fire Spirit

Once again, the Fire Spirit must be summoned to overcome gloom in an ageless dance that mirrors the eternal struggle between darkness and light.

- Will Shuster

This Page: Left: *Original Fire Spirit Jacques Cartier performs in front of the Gloom Monster in 1950.* **Above:** *Cartier taunts Zozobra in 1968.* **Opposite Page:** *Chip Lilienthal continued the Fire Spirit role, shown in 1987.*

The character who faces Old Man Gloom in the epic battle between Darkness and Light is officially known as the "Fire Spirit." He/she is often called the Fire Dancer, but that is a misnomer. Since 1939 the Fire Spirit has been performed by the following (in these years):

- Jacques Cartier (1939-1969, created the Fire Spirit character)
- James "Chip" Lilienthal (1970-2003)
- Doenika Lilienthal (1989-1991)
- Katy Lilienthal Clopper (2004-2006)
- Helene Luna (2007-2024)

vs. Zozobra

Who's going to stand up to that 50-foot monster on top of the hill? Who's going to dance at his feet while he moans and groans and thrashes about? Who's going to tease and taunt the growling gloom beast? There's only one person for this job: the Fire Spirit, Zozobra's arch-enemy. Dressed in a sparkly red costume and flame-like headress, the Fire Spirit appears magically at Zozobra's feet, armed with blazing torches ready to end Old Man Gloom's reign of terror. Let the battle begin. Zozobra must burn!

The first printed report of an identifiable character dancing in front of Zozobra was in a 1932 newspaper article mentioning a "winged fairy," a precursor to the character we know today. This was Rosina Muniz, who performed this role through 1938. Shuster intuitively knew that the dramatic burning show needed a human-scale adversary to confront and defeat the monstrous effigy. Little is known about the nature of the costume or performance, and no photographs are known to exist.

In 1939, Shuster saw an opportunity to take this character and performance to another level when he learned that Jacques Cartier, an internationally renowned professional dancer, had recently moved to Santa Fe. Shus asked Cartier to create a performance specifically for this event, something highly dramatic and visually compelling. Cartier agreed to

continued on next page

Photo Credits: Opposite Page: Far Left: New Mexico State Tourist Bureau, Courtesy Palace of the Governors Photo Archives (NMHM/DCA), #177006. Center Left: John Candelario, Courtesy Palace of the Governors Photo Archives (NMHM/DCA), #189151. This Page, Right: Sydney Brink, Courtesy Palace of the Governors Photo Archives (NMHM/DCA), #HP.2014.14.1634.

Epic Battles with

the challenge, and they created the "Pageant of Gloom and Joy" which included scores of ghostly "Glooms" (Zozobra's minions) and a triumphal dance battle with the newly created "Fire Spirit" – the "good spirit" battling that monstrous "bad spirit" on the hill. Cartier created the Fire Spirit's familiar red costume and the swaying dance moves up and down the steps below Zozobra. That costume and those dance moves will be familiar to everyone who has seen the event over the past 85 years.

Jacques Cartier performed the role of the Fire Spirit faithfully for 30 years, through sprained and broken ankles and countless burns from showering sparks. At an advanced age, Cartier knew he had to "pass the torch" to a younger dancer, and he identified as a perfect candidate a student in one of his dance classes, Jim "Chip" Lilienthal. Cartier danced that role for the last time in 1969, and in 1970 Lilienthal officially took the torch(es) and climbed those stairs to face Old Man Gloom.

*This Page: Above: Chip Lilienthal dances triumphically as Zozobra goes up in flames in the 1980s. **Right:** Helene Luna creeps stealthly towards the gloom beast in 2023. **Opposite Page: Near Right:** Luna stands defiant, showing off her traditional costume and headdress. **Far Right:** Luna confronts Zozobra with torches in 2018. She will "pass the torch" to another dancer in 2027.*

Old Man Gloom

Chip Lilienthal performed the role of the Fire Spirit for the next 33 years, from 1970 to 2003. Honoring the tradition, he faithfully recreated the dramatic and dangerous dance choreographed by Cartier, and he maintained the sparkling red costume, reinforcing the classic look and moves of Zozobra's nemesis. Chip's daughter, Doenika Lilienthal, filled in for him as the Fire Spirit for three years when he couldn't perform (1989-1991), and in 2004 when Chip was ready to retire, his other daughter, Katy Lilienthal Clopper, became the Fire Spirit for three years (2004-2006).

In 2007, the costume and torches were passed to Helene Luna, and a new era for the Zozobra-defeating Fire Spirit began. Helene had performed in the Zozobra pageant for many years as a supporting dancer under Lilienthal, so she knew the moves. Luna continued to perform the Fire Spirit role through the Centennial in 2024, staying true to the spirit and legacy of Cartier and Lilienthal as she brought new energy into the epic dance battle between Light and Darkness.

The Fire Spirit battles the darkness to bring forth light and vanquish Santa Fe's oldest foe.

— Will Shuster

Photo Credits: Opposite Page, Far Left: Mark Nohl, Courtesy Palace of the Governors Photo Archives (NMHM/DCA), #HP.2019.12.004. All other photos by Bryce Risley.

*Gloomies ominously descend the stairs, ca. 1950 (**this page**) and march under Zozobra's spell in 2024 (**opposite page**). Santa Fe kids are delighted (and lucky) to participate as Gloomies in Zozobra's annual burning event. Being a Gloomie is a rite-of-passage tradition for generations of Santa Fe children.*

Photo Credits: This Page: New Mexico State Tourism Bureau, Courtesy Palace of the Governors Photo Archives (NMHM/DCA), #HP.2007.20.1153. Opposite Page: Melinda Herrera.

Other Players

The Torch Bearers

The Torch Bearers are noted as "torch bearing townsfolk" in Shuster's description of the Pageant. They play a key role in waving their flaming torches at Zozobra's feet, which has the effect of awakening the Gloomies from their brainwashed stupor. Then they run away. The Torch Bearers have been performed by local Boy Scouts (for many years) and various volunteers from the community.

Zozobra's Voice

Zozobra has a distinctive growl, moaning and groaning as the Pageant unfolds at his feet. The appearance of each character ellicits different vocal reactions, which escalate during the Fire Spirit's dance battle, lighting of fireworks, and the ensuing blaze that consumes the gloom monster. Numerous Kiwanians have shredded their vocal chords performing the Zozobra Voice over the decades.

Ghostly 'Gloomies'

Zozobra's Gloomies are those small, ghostly, kinda-creepy, sheet-clad minions shuffling around his feet, the youth of Santa Fe locked in sadness under the spell of Old Man Gloom. Thousands of youngsters have performed as Gloomies over the years, a real rite-of-passage for kids in Santa Fe. *Imagine being part of Zozobra's show!* Terrifying perhaps, yet fun, a dream-come-true for young die-hard Zozobra fans. Their part is short, and plenty of adult Gloomie-tenders ensure they come and go safely, kept well out-of-reach of fire and the monster's long arms.

The Zozobra Orchestra

A combo of local musicians – known as "The Zozobra Orchestra" – perform live as the dramatic Pageant unfolds. Complex, multi-rythmic drums pound and pulse, guitars scream, synth keyboards howl, and horns blare into the night sky, emphasizing the drama and tragic themes unfolding around Zozobra. The music supports the movements of the pageant characters in this unique battle of gloom vs. joy.

The Animators

Unseen in the darkness behind the effigy, a group of 12 volunteers clad in fire-fighter suits bring the giant marionette to life by pulling the ropes that move Zozobra's articulated arms, head, and mouth. They "animate" Old Man Gloom as he reacts to the Gloomies, The Fire Spirit, and the fire itself. When the burning beast finally gets too hot the animators drop their ropes and run for safety.

Fantastic Fireworks Finish the Fight

The annual Burning of Zozobra is all about the battle with darkness and the astonishing fiery end of Old Man Gloom, but it starts with a dance party and ends with a spectacular fireworks show, known as one of the best in New Mexico each year. Fireworks frame Zozobra's burning, starting with a flash and a bang, then proceeding with a traditional (and Shuster-specified) sparkling Niagra "waterfall" casading from both sides towards the beast. Fireworks announce the arrival of the Fire Spirit and continue accentuating the dramatic dance at Zozobra's feet, then more rockets explode as OMG burns. The pyrotechnics dazzle everyone with a monster-worthy finale signifying the death of gloom, and they go on and on, flashing and popping, booming and blasting, surely impressing even the most cynical spectator. Everyone feels satisfied as the fantastic show concludes. The crowd claps and screams their approval, then turn and happily head home feeling oh-so-much better.

Opposite Page: Top Left: Local bands play for the crowd all afternoon and evening, creating a festive spirit prior to the burn. *Bottom Left:* The cascading "waterfall" effect closes in on Zozobra in 2013. This dramatic effect gets OMG agitated and he starts moving wildly in response. *This Page: Left:* Sparkling blasts fill the sky above an angry Zozobra in 2014. *Below:* Old Man Gloom gets backlit and provoked with dramatic pyrotechnic rockets in all colors in 2023 *(left)* and 2020 *(right)*.

Photo Credits: Both Pages: Top Far Left: Andres Maestas. Left: Marcos Herrera. Bottom three photos by Melinda Herrera.

They Build Him and

"Zozobradores" are the dedicated crews of community volunteers who have built the gloom monster Zozobra for a century. They work on the beast out of a passion to see that Zozobra is done right, that he looks good and performs well during a blazing show that hopefully satisfies the Santa Fe community.

Using plans adapted from Shuster's originals, the Kiwanis Club-led effort takes thousands of hours over many months. These "Zozobra workers" labor long and hard, but the results are gratifying: thousands of neighbors gathered shoulder-to-shoulder demanding they "Burn Him," the wide-eyed children amazed and aghast as they witness a monstrous nightmare-come-to-life, and a spectacular fiery show ending in a cloud of smoke and a pile of ashes that signify a cleansing, the start of a worry-free new year. It's a lot of work, but certainly well worth the effort.

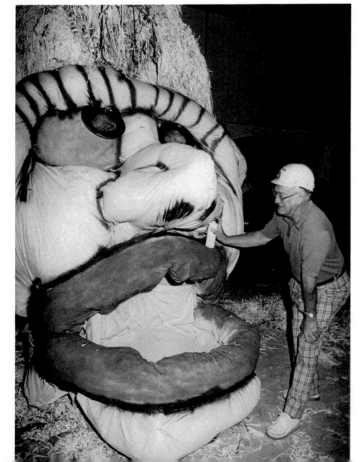

Photo Credits: This Page: Top Left: Jeff Klein, Courtesy Palace of the Governors Photo Archives (NMHM/DCA), #HP.2014.14.1943. Left: Courtesy Palace of the Governors Photo Archives (NMHM/DCA), #HP.2014.14.1626. Above: Mark Lennihan, Courtesy Palace of the Governors Photo Archives (NMHM/DCA), #HP.2014.14.1635.

They Burn Him

Zozobra's face has evolved somewhat during the last 45 years but it remains basically the same. It depends on the artist who paints him. But now we're in a position where we can't change it. It's traditional, like Santa Claus almost.

- Harold Gans, long-time Santa Fe Kiwanis Club member and the voice of Zozobra for many years, Aug. 30, 1972

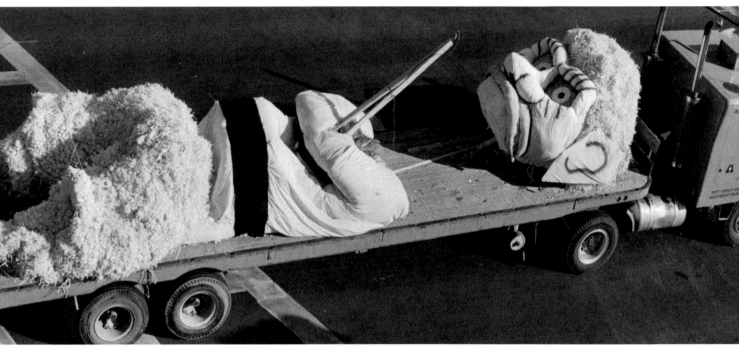

Opposite Page: Far Left: Kiwanians at work finalizing Zozobra's head and face in the 1980s and 1990s. Left: A PNM crew assists the Zozobradores in securing OMG to his pole in 1982. This Page: Top Right: Zozobra's massive head gets loaded onto a truck headed to his annual party, ca. mid-1950s. Above: The disembodied effigy takes his last ride on a big rig heading to Ft. Marcy park for his evening celebration in 1987. Right: Once at the park, the Zozobradores work to get the giant's head and body properly mounted on his pole and rigged to perform for his Santa Fe fans in the evening festivities.

How Do You Build a Giant Gloom-Beast?

The Zozobradores build the giant marionette-effigy meticulously based on plans, sketches, and models handed down and refined over the years. *Left:* Detail of a small framing model that helps guide the builders. After wooden frames for the waist, torso, and shoulders are built, flexible wire fencing is stretched the length of the body. Then, *(Below and Right)* shredded paper is stuffed in the fencing around and within the body. *Bottom Row:* Sewing Zozobra's huge cloak and sleeves requires lots of fabric and many hands. The finished fabric-wrapped beast is shown in pieces at bottom right.

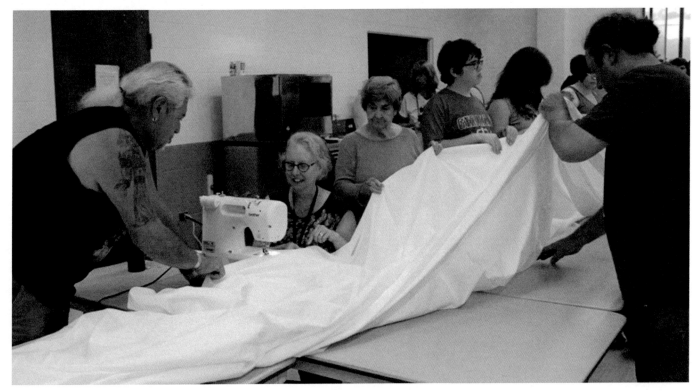

Very Carefully!

*Additional steps in building Old Man Gloom
are shown on the following pages.*

Photo Credits: Both Pages: All photos by Melinda Herrera.

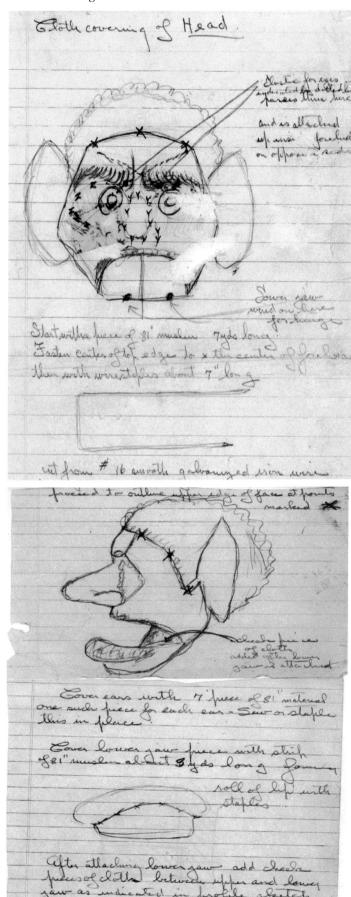

Making a Massive

Zozobra's head, hands, and arms are shown here under construction. *Top Row:* The wooden skeletal head frame is built, stuffed, wrapped, and painted. Then his eyes are attached and wired (since the early 2000s they light up). *Middle Row (Right):* Hands are sculpted with wire fencing, wrapped with fabric, then detailed. Zozobra's hands, fingers, and face evolved in the 2000s to become noticably finer and more detailed. *Bottom Row:* Zozobra's huge arms are built with wood, fencing, and fabric, then attached to the hands. Once complete and burn day arrives, the nearly 3000-pound monster is loaded onto a truck for his journey to the park, where he is hoisted onto a pole to meet his destiny later that evening.

Sketches above by Will Shuster Jr., courtesy of the Shuster Family.
Photo Credits: Both Pages: All photos by Melinda Herrera.

Marionette-Monster

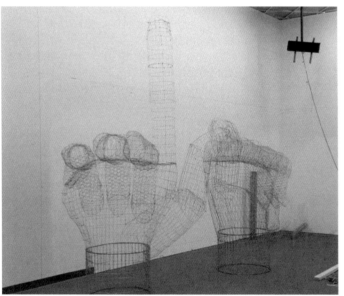
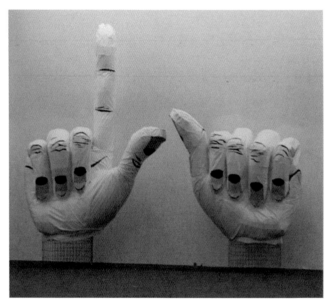
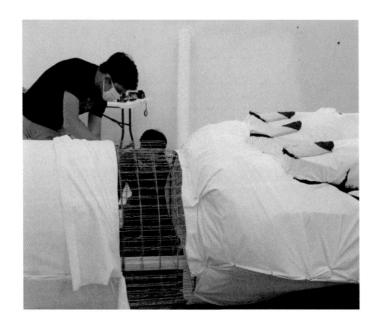

Kiwanis Club of Santa Fe Keeps

When Will Shuster knew it was time to hand off the responsibilities for his beloved Zozobra event, he didn't look far, as many of his friends and helpers were members of the Kiwanis Club of Santa Fe. As a community service organization committed to helping the youth of Santa Fe, and with years of experience helping Shus build Zozobra and run the event, the club was a good fit for staging the annual Old Man Gloom project. Kiwanis members were mentioned as participants in the earliest published report of the event (in 1926), so they were Zozobradores through and through. Kiwanis agreed, committing to take on the production of this huge and complex traditional event, and to protect Shuster's legacy. So in 1964, after trademarking and copyrighting his gloom monster, Shuster gave those rights to the local Kiwanis club, sure that his "big baby" was in good hands.

As "keepers of the flame," the Kiwanis Club has proven to be a good steward for Old Man Gloom and the Burning of Zozobra event. This group of community volunteers has steadfastly carried it forward through the years, topping Shuster's four decades with six more decades, and surely many more to come.

The Santa Fe Kiwanians are an eclectic group of local citizens who got bit by the Zozobra bug, each and every one. They meet all year, they work for months and months, dreaming and planning and building, intent on making the next Zozobra the best ever. They toil long and hard in the Spring, in June, July and August, in those final weeks, and especially during that final day -- "Burn Day" -- when they produce the most spectacular event Santa Fe has ever seen. Until next year.

These Kiwanis Zozobradores are committed to – and some might say obsessed by -- the big gloomy marionette, which they build and burn for their friends and neighbors, for rejecting gloom and restoring positivity in the community, and

This Page: Above: Kiwanis Club "Zozobradores" Matt Horowitz, Ray Sandoval, and Jacob Romero celebrate the accomplishment of getting the 50-foot tall, 3000-pound Gloom Monster properly attached to his burn pole in 2023. Below: Santa Fe Kiwanis members meet monthly to plan their numerous projects and fundraising events. Opposite Page: Dedicated Zozobradores, including Kiwanis Members and other community volunteers, move Zozobra's giant head into place.

Photo Credits: Above, Top: Bryce Risley. All other photos on both pages by Melinda Herrera.

Tradition Alive and Burning Bright

I had the Kiwanians who took the part of "Glooms" in a procession around the figure, carrying green torches and then we had a bunch of artists who were the merrymakers who came on (and chased...) the Glooms away and ignited the figure.

- Will Shuster

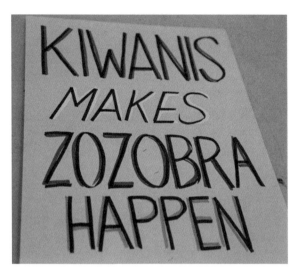

for a good cause, as all net event profits are donated to local youth organizations. It is no small undertaking, as security and crowd control issues have caused the event production to become tremendously challenging and sophisticated, like an NFL game or a large concert. They also thread a fine line in trying to meet attendee expectations of a "big show" in the new millennium with feelings of keeping it "traditional" and old school. But don't get gloomy over that, as Zozobra might want you to, because the Kiwanis Club members, those true believers, are sure to make this year's burn a good one, better than the last, completely awesome. For they understand Shuster's intentions and the crowd's expectations, they get it.

When all the hard work is done for another year, when people in that crowd are hoarse from yelling "Burn Him!" and head home, and the beast has been reduced to smoke and ash, these Zozobradores will clean up the ash and the trash and start planning next year's burn. Expectations are high in the community which loves this crazy event so much. Expectations are high among the Kiwanian OMG-fanatics as well. They want Santa Fe to have fun, to feel better with a post-burn sense of release and feelings of a fresh start. They want everyone watching to say, "That was the best burn ever!" Surely it will be, every year for the next hundred years.

The Kiwanis Club of Santa Fe has developed considerable expertise producing events during their 60 years of executing Zozobra, so much so that the City of Santa Fe contracts the Club to produce other annual events for the community, including New Years Eve on the Plaza, the 4th of July Celebration, and the Dia de los Muertos event on the Plaza.

Through their fundraising efforts (primarily the Burning of Zozobra event since 1964) the Kiwanis Club has donated over three million dollars to support the youth of Santa Fe and Northern New Mexico, mostly through grants to non-profit organizations serving youth in the community.

To change or not to change? That is a tough question always on the minds of the Kiwanis keepers of the flame for this beloved Santa Fe tradition. How does a 100-year-old event successfully move into a second century? How much does the community crowd want Zozobra to stay the same, to remain "old school" like they remember it back in the day? Does that get boring year after year, or is it comforting? Do they expect it to get "bigger and better" each year? Nostalgia and tradition are important, but do they limit the possibilities of imagination, improvement, and change? How do modern technologies and production values impact the event? Is an element of change and surprise a good thing? What would Shuster do? As an artist designing an artistic event, you might think Shus would want to change it up each year, at least somewhat, while respecting the tradition. Stay true, yes, but keep it interesting, and don't disappoint. That's the dilemma -- and the challenge -- for the Zozobradores.

It Takes a Village of Volunteers to Defeat Santa Fe's Gloom

'Fired Up' for Zozobra

Zozobra ignites passion, and passion is the soul's fuel. Once that soul fire is lit, it's hard to put out! On paper, Zozobra belongs to the Kiwanis Club of Santa Fe, but in real life, Santa Fe's most infamous citizen is a pervasive presence in the lives of countless New Mexicans.

The feelings of release and renewal that mark the Zozobra tradition were best expressed by Zozobra's creator Will Shuster, who wrote these words to a friend in 1924: "After the flames consumed the effigy, and the embers faded into the starlit Santa Fe sky, we stood together, a group unburdened. In the ashes of this effigy lay the worries of the past year, and from them, we shall rise anew, our spirits ablaze with hope and renewal. Tonight, we have not just witnessed a spectacle; we have participated in a… rite of purification, laughter, and rebirth."

The Zozobra mythology speaks to the very nature of being human: we all suffer what Shakespeare called the slings and arrows of outrageous fortune, those we inflict on ourselves and those we inflict on others. By embracing the Zozobra tradition heart and soul, we do as Shakespeare suggested—we take arms against a sea of troubles and by opposing, end them—burning our gloom as our better natures call forth The Fire Spirit living inside all of us.

Fervent devotion to Old Man Gloom starts early and kindles a fierce desire to participate. It's not unusual to see a three-year-old mirroring Zozobra's moves, and being a gloomie or torchbearer, designing a poster or tee-shirt, performing at the event, or simply volunteering to help is a lifelong badge of honor for young and old alike.

Scores of Zozobradores, volunteers, and performers work tirelessly to create a spectacular show each year. These photos reveal just a small collection of the many Gloomies, Animators, Torch Bearers, Dancers, Musicians, Kiwanians, and countless volunteers who helped stage this traditional gloom-busting, feel-good event for Santa Fe during recent years.

Photo Credits: Both Pages: All photos by Melinda Herrera.

One has only to look around Santa Fe to see the results of creative embers smoldering in the minds of gloom-burners long after Zozobra is reduced to ashes. Zozobra artifacts—a wrought iron gate, a Big Boy statue repurposed as Zozobra, Halloween costumes by the dozens, murals, art objects, and thousands of images—are exciting encounters. Meeting a fellow fan in a Zozobra tee-shirt prompts a conversation on how long they've been attending the event and what was their favorite year. And when a vintage tee pops up on eBay, it sets off a bidding war.

Online chat groups compare the merits of one Zozobra versus another even when the years under discussion were decades before chat members were born. The frenzy always peaks around the color of Zozobra's hair, a

mystery left unsolved until the event team pulls out the spray paint just before Old Man Gloom rises on his pole.

In a time when so much feels artificial and manufactured, joining together year after year to create something and then consciously destroy it for a purpose is a profoundly authentic experience, both uniquely personal and deeply collaborative. The Zozobra community welcomes everyone and that sense of belonging is also a release. Those who have a passion for Zozobra share an unshakeable bond; a connection baptized by fire that is never extinguished.

Adios, Zozobra! Burn you must and will, as long as we keep the fever of this fiery tradition burning in our hearts.

Judith Moir, *Kiwanis Club of Santa Fe*

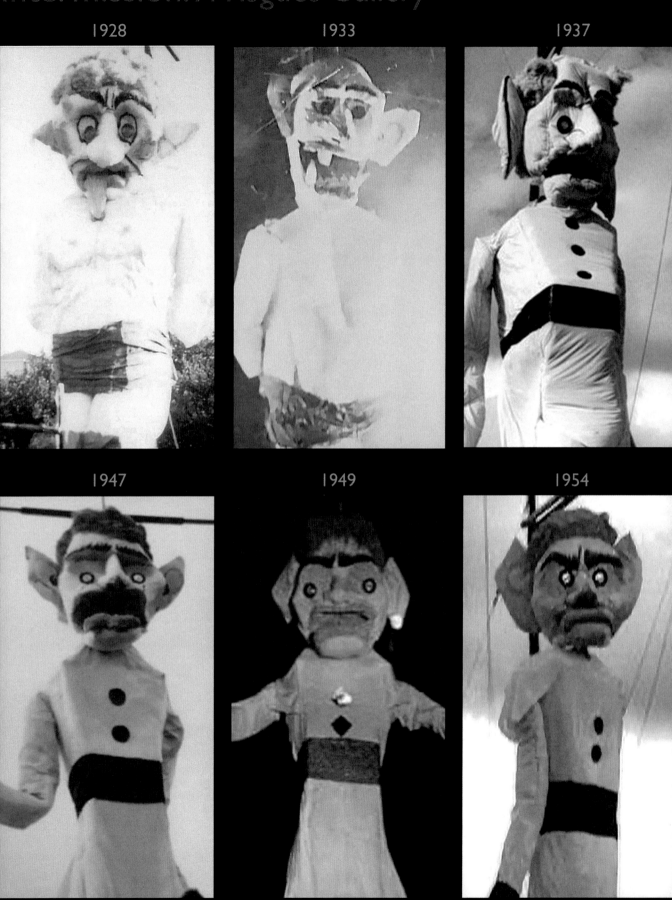

1928   1933   1937

1947   1949   1954

1998   2002   2006

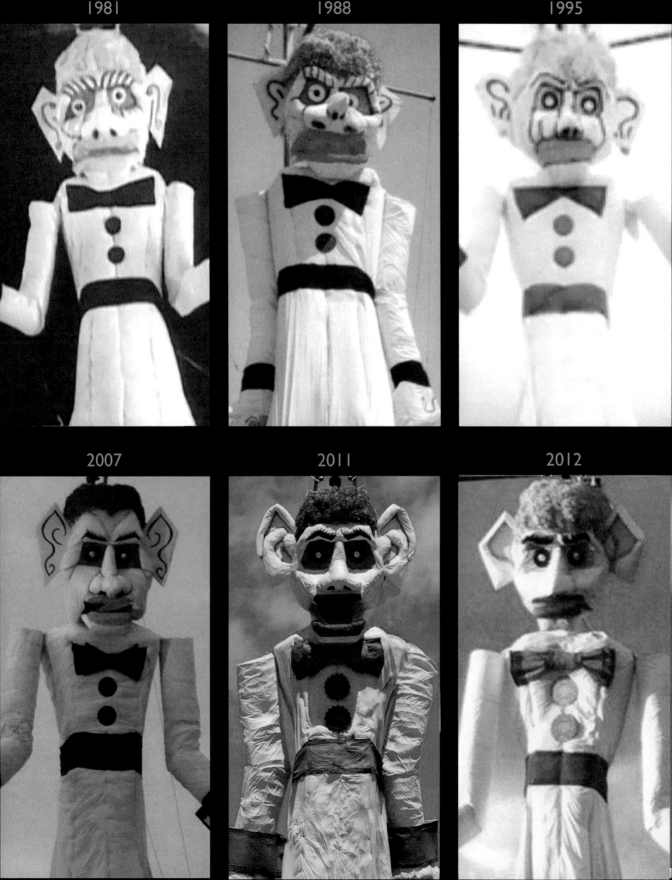

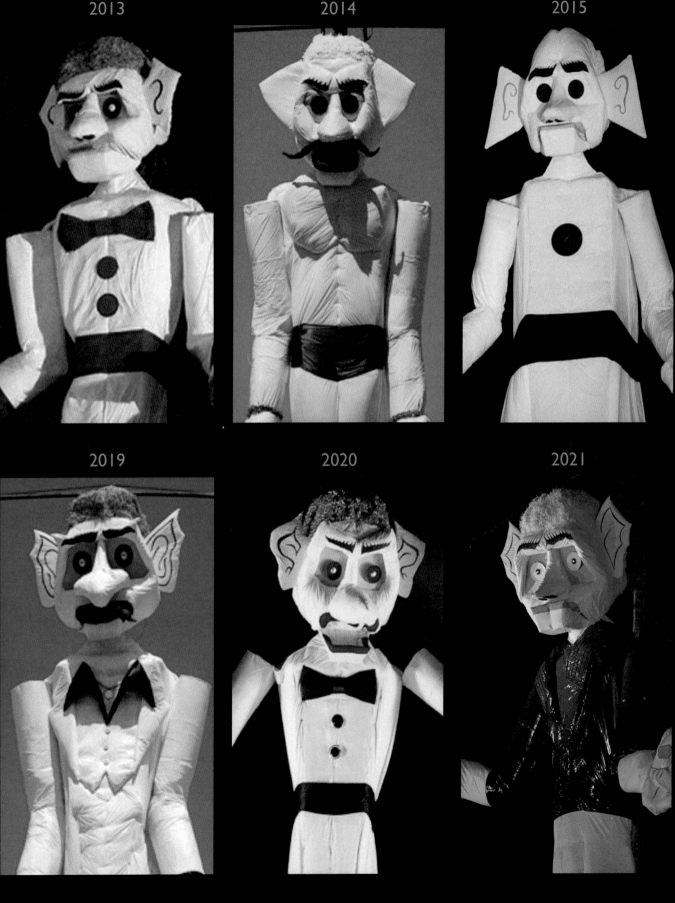

2013   2014   2015

2019   2020   2021

2016

2017

2018

2022

2023

2024

The Santa Fe community has embraced Old Man Gloom in all shapes and sizes for a hundred years, making The City Different's favorite monster an icon and its unofficial mascot.

Loving a Monster

Community 84

The Burning of Zozobra tradition bonds the community through family rituals and a shared intention to release our gloom.

Kids and OMG 90

Old Man Gloom is a Santa Fe kid's fantasy, both dream and nightmare come to life. Sounds like fun.

Zozobra and Me 94

Seems like everyone who gets around Zozobra wants to take a picture with Santa Fe's boogeyman. Say "cheese."

Photo Credits: This Page: Top Left: See page 85.
Top Right: See page 91. Above and Right: See page 95.

SF ♥ OMG

The Art of Zozobra

Around Town 98

Images of Zozobra are seemingly everywhere in Santa Fe, sometimes hiding in plain sight.

Framed 102

The imagination of Santa Fe's creatives runs wild with fantastical Zozobra imagery in all styles.

Little Zozos 112

There's no end to the variety of Zozobra images and OMG merchandise, and no bounds to the ways the big gloomy guy can be recreated on a small scale.

In the Press

NM Magazine 118

The official State Magazine has featured the unofficial State Monster periodically for decades.

SF New Mexican 126

Santa Fe's local newspaper has faithfully documented Zozobra's life and times and every spectacular fiery death for a hundred years.

Photo Credits: This Page: Top Left: See page 100. Top Right: See page 106.
Above Left Center: See page 112. Left: See page 119. Above: See page 143.

It's Unanimous: *Burn Him!*

Crowds are an essential element of the Pageant of Gloom and Joy, a crowd of Santa Feans who through the force of their goodwill, collective intention, and raucous cries to "Burn Him" inspire the Fire Spirit to put an end to Old Man Gloom one more time. And Santa Fe never disappoints in turning out a spirited crowd for the Burning of Zozobra. By nine-o-clock on Burn Night the field is typically packed, rain or shine, the crowd in a festive mood anticipating the fiery show, ready to be amazed.

Granted, not all Santa Feans attend Zozobra, many never will, and that's often because some folks "don't do well in crowds." That's understandable. And it leaves more room for the rest of us. Most years the show is sold out, late-comers turned away. Attendance may be capped at 65,000 on the field (!), but thousands more sit on hillsides, gather in nearby patio parties, or stand in the streets to watch, just close enough to feel the vibe, hear the growls, and see the fireworks. Many thousands of others watch on TV or online to experience the gloom-burning from a safe, secure, and convenient location anywhere around the world.

But the real action is in the park, on the field, standing shoulder to shoulder just a few hundred feet from the big guy, thousands of witnesses and participants in the gloom-burning, as Shuster intended.

It's a cathartic experience: the coming together, the waiting, the anticipation and restlessness. The band finishes, the National Anthem is sung, then the lights drop and the crowd cheers, glow-in-the-dark wands and lights shake across the field as the Zozobra Orchestra starts the show. The pageant has begun. The spectators crowding the field all stand now, packed together, watching in amazement as Zozobra moves and comes alive. Gloomies march and twirl, Torch-bearers sway, bonfires are lit, spotlights and fireworks illuminate the monster, then the Fire Spirit appears and dances, taunting Zozobra who shakes and groans in protest. All this as the wide-eyed crowd grows louder… "Burn Him!" they demand, participating in the show by cheering on the Fire Spirit. At last Old Man Gloom is lit, often headfirst, flames in his eyes and mouth, sparks from his fingertips. The crowd yells their approval. Each burn is unique (as fire is), sometimes his arms barely burn, sometimes it's slow in the rain. But he always burns, and the crowd stands to witness the end, cheering as Zozobra's wire frame falls where the beast just stood tall. Gloom is gone, and everyone smiles.

Photo Credits: This Page: Melinda Herrera. Opposite Page: Top: Marcos Herrera. Bottom: Sydney Brink, Courtesy Palace of the Governors Photo Archives (NMHM/DCA), #HP.2014.14.1941.

Zozobra crowds have become larger and calmer after security measures were tightened in the 2000s, now with a noticably more family-friendly atmosphere. **Opposite Page:** When the field lights finally go out, the crowd comes alive with excitement and children joyously wave their light-up toys. **Above:** The 2021 crowd is enthralled in the glow of Zozobra's red spotlights, adding to the surreal-ness of the event. **Below:** A 1980s jam-packed crowd stands ready to witness Zozobra's demise.

Community Rituals & Family Traditions

The public roasting of Old Man Gloom is an hours-long celebration of community, celebrating the possibility of new beginnings with friends and family, and with strangers. It's the Santa Fe end-of-summer, we-made-it-through-another-year, aren't-we-glad-to-be-here-in-this-great-place-together party, moving to the music and shouting "Que Viva" for being happy to be alive on this field, in this time, in the shadow of our mountain, in monsoon rain or summer shine, right here in The City Different, the City of Holy Faith.

It's both a community ritual and a fun tradition for families -- bring a blanket, bring some chairs, bring the kids, there's cousin, here's mom and dad, mi hito, mis amigos, schoolmates and neighbors, and the music's playing, let's dance. Pretty soon we're gonna see The Fire Spirit -- *Orale!* -- and Old Man Gloom is going down. *Burn Him!* Now let the fireworks light up the sky -- *spectacular!* -- and we all feel like we're five-years-old, if only for this night. Again. We came, we conquered gloom, all of us together. Life is good. *Que Viva!*

Above: Beach balls thrown into the crowd brighten the pre-burn atmosphere. Below: The entire family awaits a ride to the field, an annual tradition. Below Right: Hardy Santa Fe crowds pack the field on a rainy Zozobra night. They wouldn't miss it!

Photo Credits: Top Left and Lower Right: Melinda Herrera. Above: Veronica Trujillo.

Above: Zozobra-watchers stand in anticipation as burn-time draws near, 2018. *Below:* Zozobra fans enjoy the mood and merriment of the pre-burn festivities on the field.

Photo Credits: Top: Bryce Risley. Above: Lauren Stutzman.

Releasing Gloom:

Burning Zozobra is fundamentally about the release of the Santa Fe community's gloom, woes, anxiety, trials and tribulations. Shuster designed the ritual for the whole community to witness and participate in: First, to inspire The Fire Spirit to face and conquer the Gloom Monster by actively and loudly yelling "Burn Him," and Secondly, to project our own collective and individual feelings of gloom onto the giant effigy to rid ourselves of negativity for another year. It's the cathartic release of gloom through the astonishing burning of the effigy that gives the event its power.

While the power (in our minds) to release that gloom by simply thinking it is strong, that power seems amplified when you actually write down whatever's bothering you -- what's not working in your life, or what you want to rid yourself of – and have it placed directly into Old Man Gloom. Then you know the resultant fire and spectacle is actually feeding off your physical writing, along with thousands of others written by fellow Santa Feans.

So it's part of the collective community tradition to write down your "glooms" and stuff that paper into a "gloom box" which will dutifully be placed within the beast. Arrangements have

Writing one's "glooms" down on paper is deeply personal, and those submitted are never shared. People do report, not surprisingly, that the most common topics written for burning and "release" generally include:

- Health Issues and Costs

- Troubled or Failed Marriages and Relationships

- Finances and Finacial Hardships

- Employment and Work-related Issues

- School Problems

- Negative Feelings and Depression

- Stress and Feeling Overwhelmed

Photo Credits: This Page: Right: Andres Maestas. All others by Bryce Risley.

Write It Down and Burn It Up

even been made for online gloom submissions from out-of-towners, and the Zozobradores who manage these things make great efforts to ensure they all get burned. They are, after all, true believers, and they understand the power of burning/releasing.

Over the years folks have also brought a variety of personal items for burning: paid-off mortgages that were burdensome, divorce papers and wedding dresses from failed marriages, healthcare bills and medical records, and countless other trinkets and totems of personal pain. And for many years the bulk of shredded paper that was stuffed into OMG's body cavity for burning were old Santa Fe Police records. Now that's Karma.

It's all in good fun, sure, but when you do write down your glooms and see them burn with Zozobra, you definitely feel better.

Both Pages: *ZozoFest attendees of all ages write down their "glooms" and drop them into Gloom Boxes, which will be deposited into Zozobra himself and burned. "Glooms" can also be submitted for the burning ritual online and in-person at the event.*

Santa Fe Kids Love Zozobra

Photo Credits: This Page: Above: New Mexico State Tourism Bureau, Courtesy Palace of the Governors Photo Archives (NMHM/DCA), #HP.2007.20.1108. Below: Santa Fe New Mexican, Courtesy Palace of the Governors Photo Archives (NMHM/DCA), #136981. Opposite Page: Center Right: Leslie Tallant, Courtesy Palace of the Governors Photo Archives (NMHM/DCA), #HP.2014.14.1625. Far Right: Steve Northrup, Courtesy Palace of the Governors Photo Archives (NMHM/DCA), #010909.

Childhood in Santa Fe is unique because the Boogeyman comes to town every year! Yes… *an honest-to-goodness gigantic monster comes right into town and waves his arms and moans and groans, and we all yell at him and The Fire Spirit dances and kills him, and he's gone for another year. I saw it with my own eyes. It was scary, but my mom held me tight so I was OK.*

So the story goes for generations of Santa Fe kids. Initially terrified by Zozobra at young ages, they can't wait to see him again and again. It's as if he stepped out of our imagination, out of our dreams, maybe out of our nightmares. He fills young minds with fear and wonder and fascination. Monsters in real life. Fire and smoke and sparkling lights. Something about gloom and bad vibes. Scary and fun at the same time.

As school starts in August, serious discussions arise on the playground: What color will Zozobra's hair and bowtie be this year? How many fingers will be pointing? Will we get to see him on the truck as he rides through town heading to the park? Can we watch them put him up on the pole?

The creativity that Zozobra spawns in young minds can't be exagerated, not in this creative town. The amazing, flaming, walked-out-of-your-worst-nightmare gloom-beast so stimulates young imaginations that Santa Fe kids dream and draw and doodle and sculpt him endlessly. He may be scary but he's fun to think about, fun to draw and paint. Like any good/bad super-hero villain. He's Santa Fe's very own super-hero villain homeboy.

Since the early days, older Santa Fe kids have often crafted their own (smaller-scale) Zozobra effigies in backyards and arroyos, a good excuse to play with matches perhaps, and hopefully under the watchful eyes of their parents. Some of these kids grow up to join the Kiwanis Club and make the real monster for their friends and family, continuing the community tradition because they feel compelled to be part of it, driven to keep the tradition alive.

Some lucky kids in Santa Fe may get taken to where they build the monster, and after approaching the disembodied beast cautiously, will gladly crawl into the big body and help stuff him with the shredded paper that allows him to burn so easily. Imagine being inside the belly of Zozobra! Other kids might get a chance to participate in the ultimate Santa Fe kids fantasy and rite-of-passage: wearing a simple white sheet and being a Gloomie. Wow, to walk at Zozobra's feet and be part of the pageant, now that's where dreams and nightmares collide.

And oh what fun to go to Zozobra's burning when you are young, as you are burning with anticipation yourself *to see the gloom beast come alive when the lights dim, and the drums are beating and the Gloomies spin and sway, then the Fire Spirit who arrives to face the monster, dancing up and down the stairs, taunting him, and Zozobra looks around and moves and moans and growls, louder and louder. Everyone yells "Burn Him!" and it all seems so real -- it IS real, cause I'm standing here watching it – and the fireworks start, and Zozobra starts to burn, fire and smoke and it's all so amazing. The Zozobra monster is gone but the fireworks keep exploding, the best show ever. I can't wait to see it again next year!* That's a child's dream-come-true (forget the nightmares).

Safety Note: The Kiwanis Club of Santa Fe strongly advises to NEVER burn effigies in your backyard or a neighborhood field **due to serious fire and safety risks.** *"Leave that to us and come see the real Zozobra burn!"*

Opposite Page: Top: A giant Zozobra face atop a creative kid walks along a downtown street during the Pet Parade. ***Bottom:*** *14-year-old Ray Sandoval fashions his own Zozobra for a family burn party in 1988. Ray went on to join Kiwanis and has helped make the real OMG for most of this life. He was the Event Chair from 2012 through 2024.* **This Page: Top Left:** *Three neighborhood boys craft a 10-foot-tall Zozobra in their backyard, ca. 1966.* **Above:** *Santa Fe kids stare in wonder as the giant effigy is raised in place in 1959. They will likely return to see him burn later that evening.*

Childhood Tradition:

Photo Credits: This Page: Top Left and Top Center: Andres Maestas. Left and Above: Melinda Herrera. Opposite Page: Leslie Tallant, Courtesy Palace of the Governors Photo Archives (NMHM/DCA), #HP.2014.14.922.

Remembering Zozobra

As a native Santa Fean nearing my 70th birthday, I have been around for all but 30 years of Zozobra's existence. Although I was not fortunate enough to witness Zozobra's formative years, I have plenty of memories of his enduring presence in my life.

Traveling back in time, it was September 1967, and Mr. Alarid's sixth-grade class at Salazar Elementary School was evenly divided. Half the class was eager to witness the burning of Zozobra, while the rest were unhappy about the prospect. Marcos couldn't wait to see Old Man Gloom go up in flames to "get rid of all the bad luck hanging around this town." Monica had a differing opinion: "Everybody blames everything on Zozobra. It's not his fault my uncle forgot to put oil in his truck."

Amidst these diverse opinions, the students in my class were brimming with excitement and anticipation for Zozobra's demise. We painstakingly crafted Zozobra

puppets in class using popsicle sticks, construction paper, and Elmer's glue. Mr. Alarid used this project as a gateway to teach us about the history of Zozobra and the Santa Fe Fiesta, enlightening us about our cultural heritage.

On the much-awaited day, our families would gather in the backs of pickup trucks and station wagons, parking at Fort Macy Park for $3.00 a vehicle with picnic baskets filled with posole and tortillas. We sat on the grass and listened to the Mariachis play before evening fell, and we watched in awe and a hint of horror as the giant puppet met his fiery fate.

Another clear memory that comes to mind is when I was a teenager hanging out with my Santa Fe High School friends, checking out the burning, and later that evening walking down to the Plaza for the opening night of the Fiesta. The Fiesta had a carnival air, punctuated by the sea of humanity that circled endlessly around the Plaza. It seemed like everyone knew each other. Often, the boys

Having Fun with Santa Fe's Monster

Opposite Page: Far Left: *Santa Fe children have a great time stuffing shredded paper into the chicken-wire frame of the under-construction monster.* **Center Left:** *Gloomie-kids practice their* Gloomie march during dress rehearsal in 2015. **Above:** *Being a Zozobra "Gloomie" is a fun and unforgettable experience for these lucky Santa Fe children in 1986.*

would walk one way around the Plaza while the girls would circle in the opposite direction. The first pass would be acknowledged with a smile, the second with a wink, and the third would end with hand-holding and a mutual direction.

In later years, when I had a family of my own, I had the privilege of experiencing Zozobra's magnetic presence through my children's eyes. It must have made a profound impression on them, as evidenced by the fact that my daughter, Juniper, returned to Santa Fe from her home in Vermont to hold her wedding celebration in conjunction with Old Man Gloom's burning.

Santa Fe's Zozobra ritual is as vibrant today as ever. It continues to be a beloved and cherished part of the Santa Fe community's culture and identity.

As we approach Zozobra's centennial burning, I am already contemplating his eventual bicentennial ritual and wondering in what form he will appear in 2124.

What kind of world will Santa Feans be navigating as they burn away cares and troubles we cannot imagine today? It seems one thing is certain, however: Zozobra will stand ready to provide the ultimate sacrifice for his fellow Santa Feans, helping them release their stresses and worries to carry on in their fair city.

Will a sixth-grade class at a Santa Fe elementary school debate Zozobra's fate in 100 years? Will he still be assembled using wood, wire, and cotton cloth, or will he become a giant hologram being chased through the streets of downtown Santa Fe by a virtual Fire Spirit? Maybe it's better not to ponder these questions but rather to appreciate Zozobra's first 100 years and the comfort and service he has provided to the people of Santa Fe.

Thank you, Zozobra! Viva la Fiesta!

Andrew Lovato, *Santa Fe City Historian, 2024*

Can't Stop Smiling in the

There's no way you can be anywhere near Zozobra and not take a picture, right?! It's just too weird and wonderful -- and fun -- to resist. Here are a few examples of how OMG fans pose for pictures with the big guy.

Photo: Veronica Trujillo

Photo: Mary Askins

94

Face of Gloom

Photo: Patsy Sanchez

Photo: Scott Wiseman

Photo Credits: Both Pages: Above, Top Right: New Mexico State Tourism Bureau, Courtesy Palace of the Governors Photo Archives (NMHM/DCA), #HP.2007.20.1108. All other photos by Melinda Herrera except as noted.

95

Photogenic Gloomy

Photo: Bryce Risley

Photo: Nick Montoya

Photo: Vanessa Arias

Photo: Ben Nuci

Photo: Cassandra Cde Baca

Guy Poses with Fans

Photo: David Duran

Photo: Jamie Romo

Photo: Bryce Risley

Photo: Melinda Herrera

Photo: Daniel Clavio

Our Gloom Monster is

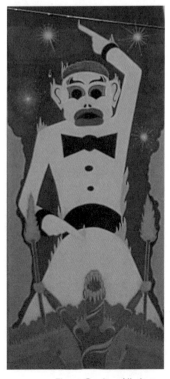

Photo Credits: All photos by Daniel Clavio.

Everywhere in The City Different

Zozobra has worked his way into the collective consciousness of the Santa Fe community over the decades, branding his gloomy self into the minds of generations. The Gloomy One has become our mascot and favorite caricature proudly identifying our unique (and "different") community. He shows up on buildings all over town, inside and out, on murals, paintings and sculptures in a wide variety of styles, expressing the dreams and nightmares of our creative community.

Opposite Page: Top: Detail of a mural at Santa Fe Place (mall), art by Monika Guerra. Bottom Left: A mural on the Santa Fe International Hostel on Cerrillos Road, art by Arnold "Rusty" Vest. Bottom Center: A mural on La Unica Cleaners on Cerrillos Road, art by Sebastian Valezquez. This Page: Above: Detail of an interior mural above the bar at the Plaza Cafe Southside, art by Robb Rael. Below: A mural at Firehouse Subs on Cerrillos Road, art by Joe Puskas.

Hard to Miss Zozobra

Above Left: *A Zozobra pinata enlivens a rustic gate on Old Pecos Trail.* **Above:** *Carved Zozobra figurines peer out of a window of the El Nicho shop in downtown Santa Fe.* **Left:** *A metal Zozobra gate by Mike Garcia looks foreboding mounted on a stucco wall in a Santa Fe neighborhood.* **Below:** *Santa Fe Fire Engine #1, which rolls from Station #1 next to "Zozobra Field," is appropriately tagged.*

in Santa Fe

Old Man Gloom can pop up nearly anywhere around town, on walls and gates, in stores and galleries, restaurants and bars, even on the road. He can't be missed, if you're paying attention. Santa Fe just loves Mr. Negativity in all forms, shapes and sizes, perhaps because we know he'll be vanquished every year.

__Top and Center:__ Zozobra can sometimes be seen driving around Santa Fe (on a license plate) and peaking from sunny car windows in parking lots and driveways. __Top Right:__ Detail on the bar top at Harry's Roadhouse shows a strange Zozobra amidst flames, art by Joel Nakamura. __Above:__ Three examples from the series of "Zozorita" glasses created for special Zozobra-themed margaritas that can be found in many bars and restaurants around town. __Right & Above Right:__ Inked images of OMG can sometimes be found on hardcore Zozobra fans. These are on the arms of Ron Martinez, longtime Head Zozobra Animator.

The Artist's Original Vision:

Zozobra's definitive image in art may be this oil painting by his creator, Will Shuster. It was painted in 1964, the year he retired from staging the event after giving the rights (and responsibilities) to the Kiwanis Club of Santa Fe. The large diptych is comprised of two panels, each 74″ by 94.25″. The dramatic, dynamic painting hung for decades in the back of El Nido restaurant in Tesuque.

Credits: **Will Shuster**, *Zozobra Mural*, 1964, oil on board, 74 x 188.5 in. Collection of the New Mexico Museum of Art. Gift of Irene Arias Walker and museum purchase with major funds donated by Margot & Robert Linton and the Los Trigos Fund with additional

Painting the Night Sky with Light

The painting was purchased by the State of New Mexico in 1992 for the collection of the NM Art Museum, and it has hung near the Governor's office on the fourth floor of the state capital for many years. The painting shows Shuster's artistic vision of "painting the sky" with fire and fireworks as the Fire Spirit confronts Zozobra, the monstrous effigy representing gloom, anxiety and negativity.

support provided by Phyllis & Ed Gladden, J. McDonald Williams, the Santa Fe Kiwanis Club, Charles & Valerie Diker, Frank & Dolores Ortiz, Helen Shuster, James S. Ipiotis, and Ray Sandoval, 1992 (1992.66.1ab). (c) Will Shuster Estate. Photo by Addison Doty.

Old Man Gloom's Monstrous Image

Old Man Gloom's iconic image began creeping into print media in the 1930s as his impact solidified in Santa Fe culture. With few exceptions, Zozobra didn't make an appearance in mass-produced posters until the 1980s and 1990s. In the early 2000s the Kiwanis Club -- as the event sponsor and copyright owner -- began publishing posters annually, as well as T-shirts and other merchandise, holding art shows and contests that stimulated artists and increased public interest in new fantastic, fun, and gloomy images each year.

*Early images of Zozobra in print. **Top Left:** Illustration by Will Shuster in the 1935 Fiesta Program. **Left:** Another graphic Zozobra illustration in the 1937 Fiesta Program. **Above:** Illustration for the 1947 "Santa Fe Fiesta Song" sheet music, signed by "Shus."*

Burns Bright in Santa Fe Culture

Left: *"Viva la Fiesta (Zozobra)" carving by Luis Tapia, 1996, in the NM Museum of Art.* **Below:** **Left:** *Art by Albert Sonnie Jaramijo, 1985. The original painting hangs on a wall at Tomasita's Restaurant.* **Center:** *"Noche Encantada" art by Amy Cordova, 2013.* **Right:** *2016 art by Russell Thornton.*

Left: **Luis Tapia,** *Viva La Fiesta (Zozobra),* 1996, carved and painted wood, 36 x 39 x 39 in. Collection of the New Mexico Museum of Art. Museum purchase with funds from the Boeckman Acquisition Fund, 1997 (1997.8.1). © Luis Tapia. Photo by Blair Clark.

Zozobra Artists Put Flames in Frames

Zozobra's haunting, scowling yet comical image -- wide-eyed and stiff-armed, fingers pointing, dancing defiantly in the raging blaze at his feet -- is burnt forever into our mind's eye. That fantastical image, along with the profound meaning behind it, provides rich inspiration for Santa Fe's many artists to interpret and express the emotion,

Left: 2019, art by Nikolas Duran-Geiger. *Below: Left:* 2015, art by David Saiz. *Center:* 2016, art by Michael Martinez. *Right:* 2015, art by Brian Gachuz.

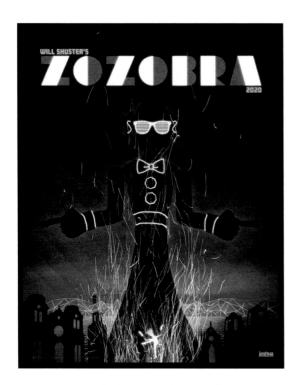

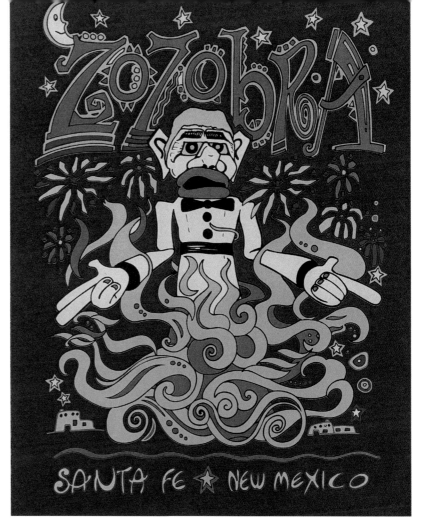

craziness, and sheer audacity of the monstrous event with drama and humor in countless styles. Throw in some flames and fireworks, a Zia sun (NM state symbol), and maybe a mountain or an adobe building, and you've got a winner. Don't forget the Fire Spirit.

Above Left: 2020, art by Joshua Gonzales. ***Above:*** *1997, art by William Rotsaert.* ***Below: Left:*** *2023, art by Nathan J. Chavez.* ***Right:*** *2016, art by Michael Martinez.*

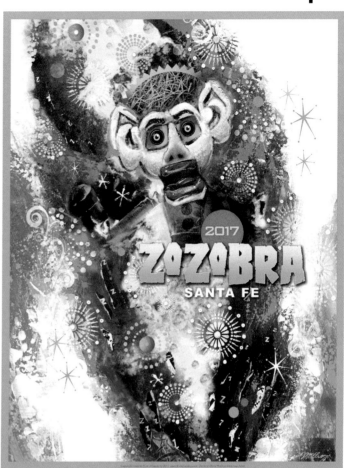

Monster Mash-ups

Top Left: 2017, art by David Di Janni. *Top Right:* 2017, art by Darlene Olivia McElroy. *Left:* 2013, art by Sebastian Valezquez. *Above:* 2022, art by Mike Graham de la Rosa.

Mean Fun for Santa Fe's Creatives

Zozobra was reimagined and "retro-fied" each year during the Decades Project (2014 - 2023), adding to the possibilities of painting our favorite monster in a variety of styles and costumes, from a stylin' disco-dancer to a raving gloom-punk to a master wizard. There is no limit to the good feelings associated with burning your gloom each year, and no limit to how we might imagine Old Man Gloom dressing up and stepping out through the years.

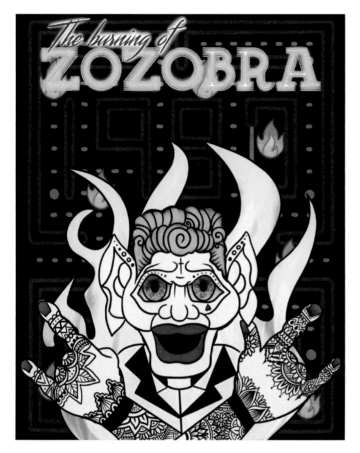

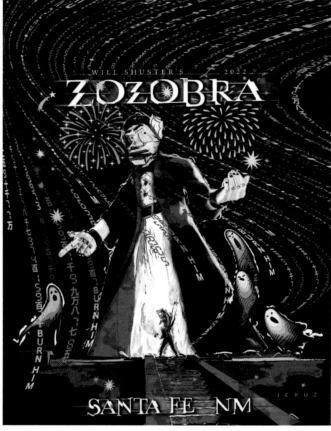

Top Left: 2022, art by Laura Moreno. *Top Right:* 2023, art by J Cruz (detail). ***Above: Left:*** 2019, art by Bradley Gard. *Center:* 2021, art by Gabriel G. *Right:* 2019, art by Virginia Asman.

THE 100TH BURNING OF ZOZOBRA
SANTA FE, NM

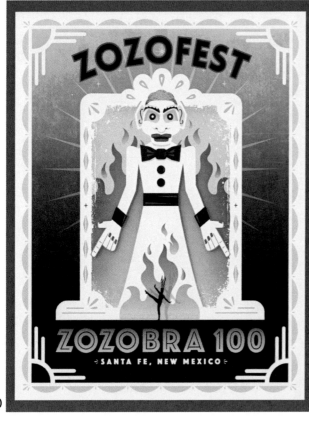

Art for Zozobra's Centennial

Zozobra's Centennial in 2024 provided numerous opportunities to create and showcase special art using OMG imagery: a show at the NM Museum of Art, the Painted Zozobra Statues Project (see pages 46 - 49), a variety of licensed products (including special beer and wine products), and of course, the official event posters, shown here. Zozobra-inspired artists have worked in a wide range of styles and themes over the years, from folky to techy, graphic to painterly, as renderings of the Gloom Monster evolve and change with the times. His image ranges from dramatic, foreboding, and scary to cartoonish and kooky.

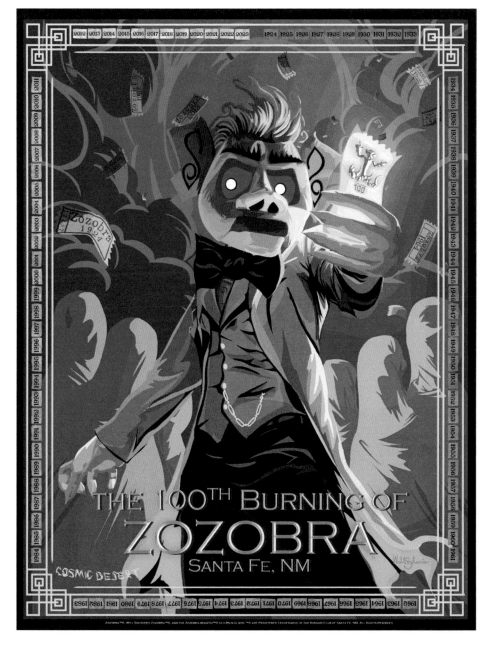

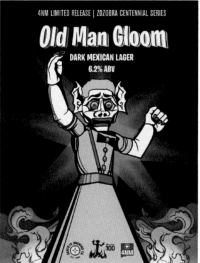

Shown are five posters created for the 2024 Zozobra Centennial, plus some 2024 licensed product labels. **Opposite Page: Top:** *Art by Robb Rael.* **Lower Left:** *Art by Anita Ashfield-Salter.* **Bottom Center:** *Art by Isaac Varela and Josiah Montoya.* **This Page: Above:** *Art by Ray Sandoval and Mike Graham de la Rosa.* **Top Right:** *Label from a special Zozobra Centennial sparkling wine from New Mexico's Gruet winery.* **Center Right:** *Two labels for specially-brewed Zozobra Centennial beers from Santa Fe Brewing Company.* **Bottom Right:** *2024 Ticket sales poster, art by Jessica Knox.*

Lots of Little Gloomie Guys

Since Zozobra's early years, the Santa Fe community has been captivated by images of the Gloomy Guy: his big eyes, the colorful bushy hair, his stiff arms, white gown with black buttons and bowtie, and that large red grimace. This iconic look has not only stimulated the imaginations of adult artists (as noted on previous pages), but youngsters seem compelled to draw and sculpt little Zozobras in myriad media and sizes. The small corn-husk dolls sold by the "Nell's Girls" club from the 1940s through the 1970s are a great example of little Zozobras spreading widely into the community. Children have been doing OMG arts and crafts projects in schools for decades, and the annual "ZozoFest" pre-burn event now provides kids with lots of opportunities to create and show their own "Little Zozos."

Photo Credits: Opposite Page: Top: Michael Heller, Courtesy Palace of the Governors Photo Archives (NMHM/DCA), #HP.2014.14.1011. Opposite Page: Pinatas, corn husk dolls, and misc. sculpture by Daniel Clavio. All others by Melinda Herrera.

Making little Zozos brings delight to kids of all ages, as seen in photos on both pages. Shown are small gloomy guys in a variety of media, including: a group of Pez covers, an elaborate Lego construction, a knit Christmas Tree topper, vintage pinatas, assorted sculptures, and magnet faces. The photo at left shows an adult group from the "Nell's Girls" club, ca. 1965, showing a variety of their little Zozobras that were sold annually as a club fundraiser. Their iconic corn-husk Zozobra dolls (below left) were designed for them by Will Shuster.

ZozoFest Presents OMG in all Forms

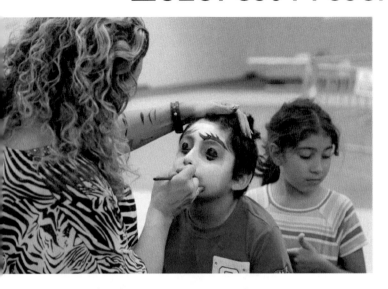

"ZozoFest" showcases many little Zozos and helps satisfy ZozoMania -- a fever that runs hot in Santa Fe in August. The annual event was started by the Kiwanis Club in 2013 as another way for the Santa Fe community to experience and celebrate Old Man Gloom. This pre-burn weekend celebration of all-things-Zozobra is an art show for artists of all ages, an opportunity to purchase the newest Zozobra merchandise, a place to write down your "glooms" and drop them into the official gloom box, and a chance to see the gloom-beast himself up close, perhaps pose for a picture with the big guy. ZozoFest officially declares that "Zozobra season" is here, and it helps the community get in the mood for the upcoming burn.

*This Page: Top: Face painting gives kids a chance to look like their favorite boogeyman. **Above and Opposite Page:** The wide variety of Zozobra-themed art is seen on display at the ZozoFest art show. **Right:** Young artist Ean Gutierrez signs copies of his Youth Poster in 2016.*

Photo Credits: Both Pages: All photos by Melinda Herrera.

This Page:
Zozobra-themed drawings, paintings, sculptures, and media of all type are displayed at the ZozoFest art show. Official posters, T-shirts, and other merchandise are also premiered and offered for sale at ZozoFest, making it a must-go-to event for Zozobra fans.

Merch and Collectables for Every Fan

Zozobra-themed merchandise has grown in number, variety, and sophistication over the last 25 years of OMG's life and death. Prior to 1999 the Kiwanis Club produced the odd poster and/or T-shirt, but in the 2000s there have been many, many products developed that fulfill Santa Fe Zozo-fanatics' hunger for OMG swag, ranging from embroidered caps and hoodies to earrings, bobbleheads and shot glasses, fake license plates and windshield sun shades. Predictably, posters and T-shirts are highly sought after and become more collectable with each passing year. The sheer variety of merchandise items offers additional ways for creative Zozobra imagery to be spread throughout the community. With no professional sports team in Santa Fe, Zozobra has become the *de facto* community team mascot, and we have the merch to prove it. *Go Zozobra!*

Photo Credits:, Both Pages: All photos by Daniel Clavio except: brown & black T-shirts on the ends by Black Duck; license plates/merch table and earrings by Melinda Herrera.

*Opposite Page: Top Left: Classic beaded Zozobra earrings have been sold for many years. **Far Left Top:** Zozobra cloisonne pins for collectors. **Far Left Bottom:** A few rare vintage Zozobra pendants. **Left Center:** An assortment of merchandise at the 2019 ZozoFest. **Bottom Rows (Both Pages):** A small selection of the countless Zozobra T-shirts produced over the years. **This Page: Above:** A group of Zozobra bobbleheads, most from the Decades Project series. **Top Right:** A rare vintage Zozobra candle. **Right:** A collection of well-worn vintage embroidered ball caps.*

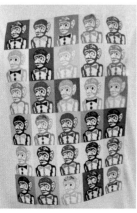

New Mexico Magazine

Zozobra, being uniquely of Santa Fe and New Mexico, came to be featured regularly in our state tourism magazine. That the giant Gloomy One is photogenic goes without saying, and of course, a picture is worth a thousand words. Though it's

Both Pages: All images courtesy of *New Mexico Magazine*, State of New Mexico Tourism Department.

Brings Zozobra to the World

hard to explain Old Man Gloom to someone -- you really have to see it to believe it, *New Mexico Magazine* helped bring his fantastical image and incredible story to the world frequently with coverage in their annual Fiesta issues.

ICE AGE BEASTS • SANDÍA HIKE • GILDED GHOST TOWN

NEW MEXICO

67TH YEAR MAGAZINE

SEPTEMBER 1989 $2.2⁵

Zozobra and his master

NEW MEXICO

MAGAZINE   AUGUST 1964 • 50 CENTS
RM
AFF.

IN THIS ISSUE
VIVA FIESTA!

Classic New Mexico Magazine *covers are shown across these two pages, from (**above, left-to-right**) 1956, 1958, 1964, and 1989. **Below:** A profile of Zozobra's creator, Will Shuster, in an article written by famed NM author Tony Hillerman in the August 1960 issue. **Opposite Page, Bottom:** A sequence of historic Zozobra photos were featured in New Mexico Magazine in 1956.*

life and it doesn't include the time spent on the preliminaries — and, if I can't pass him off on somebody else this year — it will be 34 months shot." In the last five or six years the Santa Fe Kiwanis Club has been very active in building and putting on the show of Zozobra. Shuster says that some of the main problems have been taken over by the Kiwanis, but to assure that he be on hand for the event — and the work that goes into making the monster — they made him an honorary Kiwanian. ☐ Whether or not Shuster finds satisfactory foster parents for his beast, *(Continued on Page 27)*

MEET
DR. FRANKENSTEIN
SHUSTER

BY TONY HILLERMAN

STUDIO

Magazine Features

Old Man Gloom became a statewide celebrity over the years as *New Mexico Magazine* promoted our Monster of Mayhem as a primary symbol of the Santa Fe Fiesta. While the Fiesta Council may have initially disapproved of Zozobra eclipsing their conquistadors as the go-to Fiesta brand, it's hard to argue that fire and fireworks, a burning beast, and the release of our mortal woes isn't a great way to start the Fiesta party. That's exactly what Will Shuster intended back in 1924.

Festival of the Ages

By Octavio Casavantes

IN A VAST outdoor amphitheater on the outskirts of Santa Fé, America's Oldest Capital, there will gather on the evening of September 2 some ten thousand or more persons—drawn from every state of the Union and from foreign countries—to witness an execution.

That the execution is to be achieved by burning the victim at the stake will only be cause for greater rejoicing among the spectators. The pitiable cries for mercy that issue from the doomed one will only serve to heighten the hilarity of the onlookers. And, when only a smouldering heap of ashes marks the spot where the condemned one stood, the merriment of the watching multitude will soar to a delirium of delight.

For Zozobra will be dead. Zozobra—Spanish conception of Old Man Gloom, embodiment of all human anxiety, care, woe or worry—

will have been annihilated. His giant body of papier-mache, its forty-foot length stuffed from skull to sole with every personal trouble of the whole throng of executioners, will have been burned in effigy.

Thus auspiciously—and officially—will begin the celebration of the two-hundred-and-twenty-seventh annual *Fiesta de Santa Fé*, Festival of the Ages.

While a troubled world has sought for centuries the secret of human happiness—freedom from all those things which molest the mind and harass the soul—the City of the Holy Faith has held the answer in enjoyment of a celebration which can be likened to no other on the globe.

Far from a feeling of envy toward spectacular fairs, expositions, exhibitions, carnivals and similar celebrations of great cities

Zozobra is prepared for the burning

Spanish orchestras are featured

Vargas read his proclamation

Pageantry symbolizes the re-conquest

Good-Bye to Gloom

By Anna Nolan Clark

Old Man Gloom—the Giant Zozobra

DUSK comes quickly into Santa Fé, stealing down the high peaks, shadowing sunset colors, blotting out the dancing lighted aspen trails, darkening the ground oak and piñon skirted foothills. Dusk comes quickly into Santa Fé, across the white-foamed little *rio*, along the crooked, narrow streets, shrouding the *plaza* in grey light, blurring the white-fronted houses.

Dusk comes quickly into Santa Fé, dragging its night blanket softly. Quiet holds the ancient city in the still, soft touching fingers of evening. Streets are empty. It is night.

Here in this land of mountain and cañon, of snow and desert, there is no lingering twilight, no loitering regrets of day, no languid promises of night. The sun goes out in a burst of color, lighting the peaks in a halo of flame, and night sweeps over the mountains and down into the town.

But this night is the beginning of *Fiesta*, and the hush of evening is not serene. It is charged with expectancy, with anticipation. Within the houses there is a stir of movement, a whisper of sound, and throughout the town home doors are thrown open and people surge into the streets, crowd the *plaza* and swarm up the hills of Fort Marcy.

There, rising above the town, above the heads of the people, is a gigantic, grotesque figure, Zozobra, effigy of Care, shackled and bound and

Good-bye to Gloom (Wyatt Davis Photos)

made ready for destruction. At his feet is piled a huge mound of debris, wood, dried weeds, gunpowder.

The crowd becomes restless. There are cries of "Down with Old Man Gloom." "Muera a Zozobra." "Away with Care and Worry." A dull boom is heard. Zig-zags of fire streak out of darkness and shoot into flames, curling upward, closer and closer, to the bound feet of the prisoner of frivolity who holds in his canvas covered heart all the worries of the people of the town. The crowd roars with approval, guns are fired, bells ring, whistles shrill, Zozobra's great jaws snap, his great eyes roll, and children shriek. The mob pushes back, away from the crackling heat.

Zozobra burns.

Good-bye to gloom!

Fiesta has begun. Gay, joyous *Fiesta*. *Los dias festivos*. Days of merry-making for the ancient Royal City of Santa Fé. Down in the *plaza*, bonfires of piñon and cedar blaze bright, windows shine with lamp light and fire light and house roofs are crowned with yellow *luminarias*, candles placed in bags of sand. Reflected glow illuminates the mountains, and stars hang low.

People walk about the *plaza*, join the singing groups of strolling troubadours, dance in the street the old folk dances of Spain and Mexico, and old New Mexico.

The *Fiesta* of Santa Fé is a Spanish *fiesta* and al-

An early version of Old Man Gloom

The burning of Zozobra symbolizes the destruction of all troubles and worries

IN THE YEAR 1712 the Marquis de Peñuela published a proclamation of Fiesta in commemoration of the re-conquest of New Mexico by Don Diego de Vargas.

Two hundred and some odd years later, E. Dana Johnson, who was then editor of the Santa Fé New Mexican, and I got together to hatch out a show for Fiesta.

It was not the Fiesta of the Marquis de Peñuela, but actually amounted to a revolutionary protest-fiesta, staged by the artists and writers of the community and was called *El Pasatiempo*. It was a protest against the regular Fiesta which was becoming dull and commercialized.

Between us, we worked out the general idea of the show. Dana dug up that wonderful name ZOZOBRA meaning "the gloomy one" from a Spanish dictionary, and I got to work on the details of the show with a budget of fifty dollars. That was how I innocently took the tiger by the tail.

The first Zozobra was a rather simple affair. The power company set up a pole about fifteen feet high on the lot in back of the old city hall in Santa Fé. Dan Eastman, the son of Max Eastman the writer, aided me in the work. We swathed the pole in a garment of burlap and stuffed it with excelsior that had been previously soaked in a copper sulphate solution to make green flames when it was ignited. That soaking and drying was a nasty job. I have never tackled it again.

Gus Baumann volunteered to make the head. Somehow or other Gus and I didn't get together on the scale of the figure, for when the head turned

Zozobra is FIESTA

By Will Shuster

New Mexico Magazine regularly featured articles and photographs of Zozobra, describing the astonishing event and it's link to the SF Fiesta. Promoting the monster-burning ritual and Santa Fe's historic community party was seen as a good way to stimulate tourism to NM and The City Different. Shown here are pages featuring Zozobra from New Mexico's State Magazine from the 1930s through the 1960s. Note the article above written by Will Shuster himself, August 1950.

Santa Fe's Gloom Monster

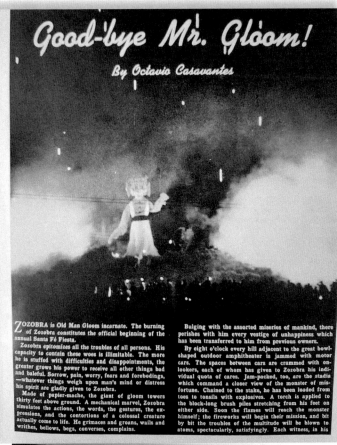

Good-bye Mr. Gloom!
By Octavio Casavantes

ZOZOBRA is Old Man Gloom incarnate. The burning of Zozobra constitutes the official beginning of the annual Santa Fé Fiesta.

Zozobra epitomizes all the troubles of all persons. His capacity to contain these woes is illimitable. The more he is stuffed with difficulties and disappointments, the greater grows his power to receive all other things bad and baleful. Sorrow, pain, worry, fears and forebodings, —whatever things weigh upon man's mind or distress his spirit are gladly given to Zozobra.

Made of papier-mache, the giant of gloom towers thirty feet above ground. A mechanical marvel, Zozobra simulates the actions, the words, the gestures, the expressions, and the contortions of a colossal creature actually come to life. He grimaces and groans, wails and writhes, bellows, begs, converses, complains.

Bulging with the assorted miseries of mankind, there perishes with him every vestige of unhappiness which has been transferred to him from previous owners.

By eight o'clock every hill adjacent to the great bowl-shaped outdoor amphitheater is jammed with motor cars. The spaces between cars are crammed with onlookers, each of whom has given to Zozobra his individual quota of cares. Jam-packed, too, are the stadia which command a closer view of the monster of misfortune. Chained to the stake, he has been loaded from toes to tonsils with explosives. A torch is applied to the block-long brush piles stretching from his feet on either side. Soon the flames will reach the monster himself; the fireworks will begin their mission, and bit by bit the troubles of the multitude will be blown to atoms, spectacularly, satisfyingly. Each witness, in his

Fiesta's for Fun
By Joe M. Clark

"**A**LL HAPPY," murmured the old Indian, Juanito, as he gazed into the crowded plaza, vibrant with color, movement and music.

His face betrayed little emotion, except for the twinkle in his eyes. But he was soon lost in the throng, his own unique garb inconspicuous among the hundreds of other colorful costumes in sight.

For this was fiesta, the Santa Fé Fiesta—fiesta incomparable. And Juanito knew the secret of fiesta, a secret his ancestors learned many, many moons ago.

That simple, wonderful secret is that fiesta is something to experience, something to feel as well as to see.

It is an adventure in happiness, as well as a spectacle. It is something remembered from a delightful dream of long ago, when the world was newer, simpler and much more fun.

Having attended their first fiesta in Santa Fé, many adult visitors depart with the impression that it simply couldn't happen and probably didn't. But children believe in fiesta much the same as they believe in Christmas. Only, fiesta lasts four days instead of just one.

Primarily a religious festival, this 237-year-old celebration contains some delightfully pagan elements. It begins the Friday evening preceding Labor Day with the

Both Pages: All images courtesy of *New Mexico Magazine*, State of New Mexico Tourism Department.

The burning of Zozobra symbolizes the underlying theme of the celebration: to throw off accumulated cares and woes and start afresh.

BY GORDON BEACH • • • • • • • VIVA FIESTA!

FIESTA time is the realization of all of the clichés so commonly tacked to New Mexico and Santa Fé. It is the time when the "City Different" is most different. It is the time when one particular part of the Land of Enchantment is most enchanting. The Fiesta of the oldest capital city in the United States is the time when all the incongruities assemble into one pulsating form which is somehow homogeneous. It is like the master blending of discordant sounds by a skilled conductor into a beautiful symphony.

Each August the people of Santa Fé partake in the

for the twentieth time they will never again work for another Fiesta, if they just make it through this one. People next year they will stay at home and sleep through the whole thing and let someone else vend the tacos and tamales.

The troupes of dancers proclaim they are fools to dance for such a small fee or no fee at all. My neighbors and I promise each other that next year we will not go to the trouble of filling the hundreds of paper sacks with sand and candles to make bright luminarias with

Tall Gloomy Guy Sells Fiesta

TURNING BACK
THE CALENDAR
236 YEARS

for

Santa Fe

Fiesta – SEPT. 4 - 5 - 6

1948

Anybody in the world can come to Santa Fé at FIESTA time and take part in the observance, and, in fact, is liable to. You will see people from everywhere, watching the destruction of Old Man Gloom, taking part in the Pet Parade, enjoying the historical pageant, attending mass. The FIESTA is an expression of the people's happiness and thankfulness for the good things of life which have come to them through the courage and energy of their predecessors in the "Land of Enchantment". Come one, come all. You are welcome!

**CITIES SERVED BY
SOUTHERN UNION
IN NEW MEXICO**

Albuquerque (City Gate), Artesia, Belen, Bernalillo, Carlsbad, Clovis, Dexter, Farmington, Hagerman, Lake Arthur

Las Lunas, Loving, Lovington, Portales, Roswell (City Gate), Santa Fe, Tesuque, Texico, Tucumcari

Southern Union Gas Company
HELPING BUILD NEW MEXICO

Zozobra was prominently featured in several advertisements in *New Mexico Magazine* in the late 1940s and early 1950s, and why not? While basically a gloomy guy, he's associated with celebration and merriment, fun and fiesta and The City Different. What business wouldn't want to be associated with all that good will?! Nowadays the Zozobra image is closely guarded -- care-tended perhaps -- by the copyright owners (Kiwanis Club of Santa Fe) to protect the integrity of the OMG brand. As innocent as they seem, it's doubtful that ads like these would be permitted in today's IP-conscious world.

Fiesta is Gay!

and the World
is Invited!

September 2 - 3 - 4 - 5

Santa Fé Fiesta is a people's observance. It reflects the people's thankfulness for their well being in a new and strange land. Its program includes parades, exhibits, social affairs, and religious rites. It is a time for people to express their happiness and renew their faith, and everybody is invited!

**CITIES SERVED BY
SOUTHERN UNION
IN NEW MEXICO**

Albuquerque (City Gate), Artesia, Belen, Bernalillo, Carlsbad, Clovis, Dexter, Farmington, Hagerman, Lake Arthur

Las Lunas, Loving, Lovington, Portales, Roswell (City Gate), Santa Fe, Tesuque, Texico, Tucumcari

Southern Union Gas Company
HELPING BUILD NEW MEXICO

Fun in Magazine Ads

The burning of Zozobra is symbolic of burning your cares and woes

Your Troubles Go Up in Smoke!

Fiesta is not only a holiday for fun, but a revival of the spirit. The burning of [Zozobra] symbolizes the shedding of your cares and worries of the past year. Your troubles go [up in smoke]
when Zozobra is burned.

Whether you live in New Mexico or in distant climes, you'll enjoy a visi[t to Santa Fe]
during Fiesta.

*Your financial troubles will go up in smoke when you use the ser[vices]
of your local banks. The banks of Santa Fé offer their services in [help-]
ing you establish a home or business in Santa Fé.*

The First National Bank
OF SANTA FE
Member FDIC

Santa Fe — Los Alamos

Santa Fe Na[tional]
Member
L. C. WRIGH[T]

Santa F[e]

NEW MEXICO Magazine

Both Pages: All images courtesy of *New Mexico Magazine*, State of New Mexico Tourism Department.

The pages shown here illustrate how Zozobra was enlisted to sell a variety of services, including natural gas, banking, and electricity in these Fiesta-themed ads in New Mexico Magazine, *ca. late 1940s and early 1950s.*

Conquistadores as of old

**242nd Annual Fiesta
Sept. 3-4-5-6, 1954**

Life is More Fun in Santa Fe

The annual Fiesta is one reason why life is more fun in Santa Fé. (There are many reasons: Climate, pleasant working conditions, charming surroundings, friendly people, and modern facilities.)

When Zozobra is burned on the opening night of Fiesta, signalling the end of woes and cares, Santa Fé begins a four-day period of celebrating that is both a time for joyous merry-making and a period for renewal of faith, for revival of the spirit.

It's good to be in Santa Fé at Fiesta time.

It's fun, too, to live in Santa Fé the year 'round, and enjoy the advantages of modern living with dependable, economical electric service. The Public Service Company of New Mexico helps to make living in Santa Fé more pleasant every day of the year.

"Go Modern—Go All Electric"

PUBLIC SERVICE COMPANY OF NEW MEXICO

Serving
LAS VEGAS — SANTA FE — BERNALILLO — ALBUQUERQUE
LOS LUNAS — BELEN — DEMING

With the Finest in Electrical Service

Magazine Confirms: New Mexico Loves

THE BURNING OF ZOZOBRA

PHOTOS BY JEN JUDGE

Nothing distinguishes Santa Fe as the City Different more than Zozobra, the 50-foot-tall puppet first created in 1924 and constructed annually to be burned before roaring crowds of thousands, taking attendees' gloom, fuss, bummers, and grief along with him. Even amid all of that fire and grim-stone, 2014 promises to bring a rebirth of Old Man Gloom's special day.

The beloved annual event was doused with some buckets of buzzkill in 2012: a ticket uptick to $20 and a kibosh on strollers that left parents feeling snubbed. The resulting backlash (and attendance drop) spurred organizers to re-tweak. In 2013, tickets were attractively priced at $10, and strollers were welcomed. And this year, for the first time since 1998, Zozobra will feel the heat on Friday night, not Thursday, which is sure to boost already robust attendance.

Tradition holds that you will still be able to burn away your worries by depositing them into a "gloom box"; meet your old friends (and make some new ones) on the Fort Marcy ball field; boogie before the burn with the variety of bands on the main stage; and buy some Zozo-themed souvenirs to commemorate the evening. If you have small children, you can opt to watch the burning on a large screen in a family-friendly area. All these changes will be orchestrated by a larger (and friendlier) security force tasked with making Zozobra a smoother and overall more cathartic experience for all. Feel the burn.
—Rob Wilder

38 NEW MEXICO | SEPTEMBER 2014

nmmagazine.com | SEPTEMBER 2014 39

Fact vs. Fiction: In Christine Barber's mystery *The Bone Fire*, heroine Lucy Newroe attends the burning of the 50-foot tall marionette known as Zozobra, a real-life event that kicks off La Fiesta de Santa Fe. This year's burning of Will Shuster's Zozobra will be September 9, at Ft. Marcy Park.

124

Zozobra

As Old Man Gloom matured into his 100-year-old self moving towards his centennial birthday in 2024, *New Mexico Magazine* continued to highlight the Grouchy One to it's national audience in the 21st century. The beloved Santa Fe character and his amazing burning event is a classic "New Mexico True" cultural institution, and our state magazine shared the weird-and-wonderfulness with the world: the giant effigy, the fire and fireworks, the crowd and the joy it brings to so many.

These pages from New Mexico Magazine *show how the state publication has continued to spotlight our love of Zozobra in the 21st century.* **Left:** *Taking Zozobra selfies in 2013.* **Below:** *A great photo sequence showing four stages of OMG's fiery demise in 2009.* **Right:** *A double-page spread of Zozobra in his glory, 2022.* **Bottom Right:** *An attendee drops his written "gloom" into a "gloom box" which will soon be placed inside the beast for burning, 2022.*

Both Pages: All images courtesy of *New Mexico Magazine*, State of New Mexico Tourism Department.

Zozobra does not go gently into the night. The marionette's theatrics and pyrotechnics are all part of the drama.

BURN, BABY, BURN!

At Santa Fe's annual Burning of Zozobra, people come together to let go of their individual disappointments, gripes, troubles, and all-around bad vibes. Let the party begin.

BY JULIA GOLDBERG

PHOTOGRAPHS BY TIRA HOWARD

47

Local Newspaper Reports

SANTA FE NEW MEXICAN
THE SOUTHWEST'S OLDEST NEWSPAPER, FOUNDED IN 1849. PUBLISHED IN OLDEST CAPITAL IN AMERICA, THE ANCIENT CITY OF THE HOLY FAITH, AT THE END OF THE SANTA FE TRAIL

SANTA FE, NEW MEXICO, SATURDAY, SEPTEMBER 3, 1932

PRICE FIVE CENTS

BURNING ZOZOBRA USHERS IN FIESTA

1932

1926

PASATIEMPO BAILE CROWDS ARMORY, ZOZOBRA IS BURNED

WITH MARCY STREET A SOLID MASS OF PEOPLE FOR A BLOCK WATCHING THE OBSEQUIES OVER ZOZOBRA, THE MONSTER GLOOM CONDEMNED TO BE BURNED AT THE STAKE, AND THE ARMORY PACKED TO THE DOORS AT THE GRAN BAILE DEL PASATIEMPO LAST NIGHT, THE OPENING NIGHT OF THE CARNIVAL WAS ALL THAT COULD BE DESIRED.

1928

Zozobra Looms Forty Feet in Air; His Head Defies Flames

Rising 40 feet in air, as he was elevated to the top of a tall pole, his vast hands waving spectrally, Zozobra, the giant effigy of Old Man Gloom, had a hard time getting burned to death on the city hall lot Saturday night. A roar

1932

ZOZOBRA HOLOCAUST HUGE; PROCESSION TO CROSS MOST DRAMATIC, BEAUTIFUL SIGHT

Fiesta Spectacles Extraordinary; Candle Parade Most Impressive Ever Held; Hundred and Fifty Children Enter Pets in Animal Fair; La Fonda Crowded With Customers at Brilliant Conquistadores' Ball, Featured by Unusually Excellent Entertainment Program

A sheet of flame a block long and a hundred feet high crisscrossed with streaking blue and green and red fireworks shot skyward on the city hall lot Saturday night, to the tune of the deafening rattle of explosions and amid the cheers of thousands as Zozobra, Old Man Depression was consumed and the 220th annual Santa Fe Fiesta was on

1936

Viejo Gloom Es Muerto; Q

Doomed foe of Fiesta on his funeral pyre as firmament is lit with lurid glare of holocaust; weeds, oil, wood, canvas, gunpowde and imagination of Artist Will Shuster combine to make thrilling spectacle.

1932

FUNERAL GONG TOLLS END OF GLOOM; BAILE AT LA FONDA

Flames Consuming Old Man Depression Will Mark Opening of 220th Annual Fiesta in the Ancient City; Marks Reconquest of Santa Fe; Great Hotel Turned Over to Merry Makers for Tonight; Procession to Cross of the Martyrs Sunday Evening

The deep boom of an immense funeral gong will herald the forthcoming obsequies of Zozobra, Old Man Depression, who is to go up in a vast conflagration and fireworks eruption tonight on the city hall lot, opening the 220th

Fiesta Fun, Fire, and Monster Sightings

The Santa Fe New Mexican faithfully reported the new fiery Fiesta phenomenon in the early days, and ever since. The local newspaper even got in on the fun by occassionally running articles about Zozobra hiding in the hills and narrowly avoiding capture.

1932

WILD EYED MONSTER, ZOZOBRA SEEN BY FARMERS NEAR NAMBE

The wild chase for Zozobra, the red-eyed monster Depression, goes on apace.

The New Mexican received the following message today from Cyrus McCormick, Jr., dirt farmer of Nambe: "Several farmers saw Zozobra crossing my place Tuesday night but the consensus of opinion is that he is really no more ferocious than the kind of grasshoppers we have already repelled. He is self-conscious, fed up, fat-cheeked and flabby, bushy-browed, broad nosed and inclined to talk out of turn. If you catch him, and burn him Saturday

the festivities and possibly smash a lot of furniture.

STAYING IN VEGAS?

Las Vegas, N. M., Sept. 1—Amid the welter of false rumors, some incline to credit the story that Zozobra, as reported, is hiding in the rear of the Las Vegas Optic office, but it is believed by less excitable people that some one merely saw Hub Kane coming out of the office and thought he was Old Man Depression because of the effect the political situation has had on him.

Mr. Kane's features as is well known bear no resemblance to the bizarre lineaments attributed to Zozobra, whose face is reliably declared

1938

Your Weeds Are Needed By Zozobra

+ + +

Have you any weeds? Not just a few weeds but lots of weeds. If you have, the Santa Fe Fiesta Council wants them.

The weeds will be used to help burn Zozobra, Old Man Gloom, on the opening night of Fiesta, Sept. 3. To make it a big blaze, weeds in great quantities are needed.

The state penitentiary will cut them and haul them. But the weeds must be within reasonable distance and must be in BIG numbers. If you have a small patch, don't call the Fiesta Council. Obviously weeds in small patches aren't wanted. But if you have a lot of them in one place, call 1492.

1932

Dread Monster Zozobra Rumored Seen in Prairie-Dog Sector and Homesteaders Are Terrorized

The homesteaders northwest of town are spending sleepless nights since the report that Zozobra, better known to the world as Old Man Depression, has been seen in that part of the country.

Barbed-wire entanglements are being erected by many of the settlers to preclude the possibility of a surprise attack.

Joe Bakos while hunting rabbits yesterday, reported seeing a huge shape crashing through the brush about two hunderd yards from where he was hunting. He aimed carefully and discharged a load of number seven shot at the dread monster, which emitted a blood-curdling cry and dashed off through the pinons. It is not known whether Mr. Bakos seriously wounded Zozobra.

These clippings from The Santa Fe New Mexican *show how the burning of Zozobra was reported in the early days. On the opposite page, headlines and articles note the spectacular nature of the event. The three articles at left show the newspaper having some Fiesta fun by reporting sightings and near-captures of Old Man Gloom, who was allegedly running loose and scaring people. Note the public request for weeds, above. Used for decades, huge piles of weeds -- preferably tumbleweeds -- were mounded high below Zozobra (shown in the early photo at left) to create a massive blaze. The article below shows how WWII impacted the burning.*

1932

International Villain Reported Near Santa Fe; Big Search On

Positive rumors have been heard about Santa Fe during the last few hours, that Zozobra; that deep-dyed in the wool villain better known to us all as Ole Man Depression, has been reported hiding in an arroyo northwest of Kitayawee.

The city fathers have commissioned Will Shuster to round up and destroy the rascal. General Osborne Wood has ordered two troops of cavalry, a machine gun battalion and a battery of field artillery also his goat herder to report to Shus at Kitavawee.

Jesus Baca and a large posse of deputy sheriffs are combing the Buckman valley in an effort to drive

State Game Warden Senor Barker may be seen scouring the countryside.

Warden Swope has been directed by Governor Seligman to prepare a special chamber in the state penitentiary to receive the guest should he be captured.

Dan Ortiz is censoring all R. F. D. mail with the hope of obtaining a clue as to his whereabouts.

President Hoover has just sent a communication from the White House demanding that Old Man Depression be taken dead or alive.

Billy Hesch the New Mexican's war correspondent in the field, reported that in an interview with Shus this morning, he had said "If I catch this

1942

Zozobra Gets Hour Reprieve From Burning

Old Man Gloom's Incineration to Come Later Because of War

Amid the shrieks and groans of all the "glooms" in Santa Fe, on a blazing funeral pyre erupting flashes of noisy fire, Zozobra, the monstrous figure who was created by Artist Will Shuster to represent "Old Man Gloom" in person, will meet his timely end as the 230th Santa Fe Fiesta gets under way on Saturday, Sept. 5.

1959

NTA FE, NEW MEXICO, FRIDAY, SEPTEMBER 4, 1959   Price 10 Cents

Gloom Vanishes Tonight With Burning Of Zozobra

Newspaper

By the late 1930s, Zozobra was solidly established as a Fiesta tradition and firmly embraced by the Santa Fe community. The idea of burning one's gloom each year was too good not to love. Reports in *The Santa Fe New Mexican* confirm that the event grew in the 1940s and 1950s as thousands of people came to witness the annual gloom-busting event.

*A folksy post-WWII editorial (**bottom left**) highlights the burning in 1946. At far right are several articles from 1960 that continue the newspaper's series (started in the 1930s) about hunting for Zozobra in the mountains near Santa Fe. Other articles feed the public's endless fascination with OMG, despite the limitations of night photography.*

1953

Photo by Art Taylor Copyright © 1953

1946

Editorial
Zozobra Es Muerto

Well folks, you can go ahead with Fiesta, because we burned Zozobra last night.

At least we burned Zozobra's skeleton, and it's really much harder to burn down a solid hunk of telephone pole than a dummy stuffed with excelsior and gunpowder.

It was all John Sloan's idea, and Will Shuster and John Hay thought it was wonderful, so we forgathered on the hillside with a can of kerosene, a pile of pinon kindling and good spirits.

Zozobra—or maybe it was Calla Hay or Oliver La Farge—groaned unhappily as we piled the kindling around his bony feet. And John Sloan suffered a twinge of conscience.

"I know it was my idea," he said. "But do you think we ought to do it?"

"We will have no mercy on the rascal," said Shus, firmly throwing his straw hat on top of the kindling pile and hauling out a match. "Zozobra must burn."

And that was the way it was.

He died hard. It took half the night and some tugging on the guy wires, but he finally came tumbling down—as dead as any Zozobra ever was. And if you don't believe it, you can go up above Magers field and see for yourself.

Afterwards we went home and made snide cracks at some very nice guests who tended to think the whole thing was kind of silly for a bunch of grownups. They'd flown out from New York to make a picture story of Fiesta and were sorry there wasn't more to it.

Well, maybe there isn't much story this year, but so far as we're concerned, Fiesta is now official.

"Zozobra es muerto. Que vivan las fiestas."

15,000 See Zozie Burn

1948

1952

Documents Annual Zozobra Burnings

1956

E NEW MEXICAN ★ ★

SANTA FE, NEW MEXICO, FRIDAY, AUGUST 31, 1956   Price 7 Cents

Meets Doom Tonight

Zozobra To Mark 30th Anniversary

OLD MAN GLOOM meets his fiery doom at 8 o'clock tonight in Fort Marcy Park for the noisy and official opening of the 1956 Fiesta de Santa Fe. The Plaza streets were blocked off today with carpenters rushing completion of the traditional food and refreshment booths, and the annual invasion of Indians from as far as Arizona reached its peak. The Indian Market along the Palace of Governors portal was jammed with assorted tribesmen in full Fiesta finery and the crowd of tribal craftsmen was assembling to offer choice sidewalk locations.

Residents get their traditional preview of fun to come last night with the annual "Kool Shoe" held atop the Kunar Town sleeping center. An estimated 7,000 gathered to hear the Mariachi Chapula warm up for their Plaza appearances throughout the three day festivities.

Fiesta Program

Here's the official program for Fiesta activities for Saturday and Sunday.

SATURDAY

10 A.M. La Parade for the Niños (Children's and Pet Parade) Assemble at Seth Hall at 9 a.m. Route: Seth Hall west to Grant, Grant north to Kurth Alley, Kurth Alley to San Francisco Street, San Francisco to Sheby. Shelby north to Palace, Palace West to Lincoln, Lincoln north to Seth Hall for refreshments and disband. Judging of prizes will take place preceding the parade at assembly point.

11 A.M. Plaza entertainment. Mariachi Chapula, The Troupeens. Music. Dancing on platform in the Plaza

Cartier To Dance To Zozobra's Demise Manana

crackling fireworks, Fiesta is at Ft. Marcy Park as in the gov-ered officially opened. The glory begins at 8 o'clock. The devotion in which Zozo-bra—the total of glory, Cartier-bra is confined and the fireworks the night of glory, Cartier-box is inaugurating the night of gold left of joy her traditional somewhere dart of glee celebration.

Eva booth, 4 ball-shoe; and calico, every drunkban and a cloud of flames will performed more...

Amelia and Marcella Mon-teza, Evano diminuer, George Geo-metza, Albert Sanchez and city Eddy and Danny team. Both dances are to be performed

with the Mariachi Chapula learn-ing. Luis Guerrera's orchestra plays at Seth Hall for the siesta Saturday, and Sunday for the Del-Valpos Ball and Monday night by the Roundup is Bailes, a series of the Betty Quena and Dorothy Park monies also public from "Mr. Vicenti's home stadium of the Betty team, Teste Ugalda, Jean-Correa, Bedilla Gallegos

Julio Alcilla Romeo, Mary Sa-dist Gonzalos, Ismale Baca, De-Berni, Retica Abeyta, Georgia Bandel, Zampbrosa Montoya, Bet-

1952

1955

10A THE NEW MEXICAN   Sunday, September 4, 1955

Up In Smoke

ZOZOBRA'S DOOM—Old Man Gloom, authored by Will Shuster and this year constructed by Kiwanians under the direction of Arch Hurlord, went up in a cloud of glory Friday evening to set a spectacular pace for Santa Fe's 244th annual Fiesta. The sequence shots by staff photographer Dick Goehring above and at left show the transition from the stark figure of the Old Man to the ashes...

1960

Zozobra Last Seen In Santa Fe Canyon

The New Mexican staff photographer has gone off on a quest for the monster, Zozobra, to get exclusive photographs and perhaps an interview with the gloomy visage.

He became intrigued with the idea of searching out Zozobra's lair after the giant, perhaps in a fit of loneliness, was seen last night attempting to carry off The New Mexican's city-bred statue, Wrong Font.

stake—a fitting punishment for a monster so heartless he would seek to spoil the Fiesta celebration.

He was sighted last night tampering with Wrong Font by New Mexican mechanic and art specialist B. Ziegenfuss. He fled when the intrepid Ziegenfuss swore at him in a Texan accent.

Zozobra was tracked to the entrance of Forbidden Santa Fe Canyon by a trail of buttons, belt buckles and auto remnants belong-

1960

11th Year, Issue No. 237   28 Pages   SANTA

EXCLUSIVE PHOTOGRAPH — A New Mexican photographer, heedless of the warnings of his friends and the encouragement of his enemies, sought out the hidden lair of the "Zozobra," or Gloom monster, yesterday and shot this exclusive photograph, losing his hat and a dozen expensive flash bulbs in the process. Monster Specialist Will Shuster has been given directions on how to reach the lair, around which he will set traps for the beast's capture.

Photographer 'Risks His Life' As He Gets Picture Of Zozobra

A New Mexican photographer thus escaped the terrible fate which certainly would have ... He took the afternoon off today... escaped with life, limb, and

1960

THE NEW MEXICAN ★ ★

111th Year, Issue No. 238-20 Pages   SANTA FE, NEW MEXICO, FRIDAY, SEPTEMBER 2, 1960   Price 10 Cents

Zozobra Trapped Near Reservoir

Santa Fe artist and Monster Expert Will Shuster announced today that he has captured the Abominable Generous "Zozobra" in a trap placed near the reservoir and outside the monster's hidden lair in the tangles of Forbidden Santa Fe Canyon.

The 80-foot monster, scream-ing, kicking and labelling Sham-es with unprintable epithets, was loaded into a big flatbed truck and carted to Ft. Marcy Park. A group of daredevils from the Public Safety Com-pany have been working all day to secure him, for the stake, where he will be on public dis-play until his execution at 8 P.M.

According to local legend, "Zozobra"—which family trans-lated, means Old Man Gloom—scrounges about town during the rest of the every sort of distress and dismay and generally giving people reason to feel un-fortunate. Each year since 1926 Shuster has managed to capture Zozobra in time to save the Ancient City from his depreda-tions during the four days of Fiesta.

Tonight, most of the town's citizens and many visitors will obey the Bacchanalian rites of Jacques Cartier and the Little Gloomy so they increase the Gargoyle-faced beast in his final throes of death.

He has been fed nothing but fireworks since his capture, which he has consumed with his utmost unsophisticating gluttony. They are expected to explode in a glory of flame and corruption when Cartier touches a flaming
(Continued on Page Two)

129

Newspaper Confirms:

Santa Fe kids can't seem to get enough of Old Man Gloom, as shown in these clippings from the *Santa Fe New Mexican*. Whether loving a Zozobra dolly or building little OMG effigies, kids growing up with Zozobra show great enthusiasm for the giant gloomy guy... and it's all great fun.

E NEW MEXICAN Santa Fe, N.M., Thurs., Aug. 31, 19

NEW MEXICAN Youth

1972

Focus: Zozobra Jr.
Bringing Fiesta home

2001

1982

Chris Romero, first place winner in the 11-year-old category.

Anita Morales, above, grabbed first place in the 8-10-year-old division and Johnny Martinez, right, was first among the 7-year-olds in the mini-Zozobra contest, part of the Fiesta Week activities.

Photos by Mark Lennihan

Little Zozobras not gloomy
79 youngsters create miniature versions of the monster

Nearly 80 Santa Fe youngsters took part Thursday in the fourth annual mini-Zozobra contest, sponsored by the Western Bank of Santa Fe in conjunction with

ranged in size from one to three feet. A few models had to be disqualified because they exceeded three feet, the maximum permissible height.

School made Zozobras as class projects.

The names of three winners in the contest were announced Thursday afternoon during a

Kids Love Zozobra

1955

Nell's Girls Again To Sell Zozobras Made From Pattern Given By Shuster

This Fiesta season will mark the *th year that Nell's Girls have* furnishing materials and making bandages for welfare patients. Those who wish to burn their

→ TRINA NORDSTRO daughter of Mr. an ert Nordstrom, is as Girls in the advance iature Zozobras. W red bandana dress, agreed that Zozob derful and announ

2006

2007

These photos from The Santa Fe New Mexican *show the many ways Santa Fe children have embraced Zozobra over the years (often literally). Building -- and sometimes burning -- small-scale Zozobras is common, as is dressing in a Zozobra costume for Halloween or the Pet Parade. But nothing is better than helping build the beast or being a real Gloomie.*

Zozobra Children audition to be part of burning celebration

2010

1975

ZOZOBRA'S RETURN—Harold Gans, left, of the Downtown Kiwanis Club is at it again, constructing the huge Zozobra for Fiesta weekend. Gans annually heads up the construction of the replica for the burning of Old Man Gloom to open Fiesta weekend. The burning will be Friday night at Mager's Field.

131

'All Things Zozobra' Found

Let your troubles go up in smoke with Zozobra

1984

1963

Taking the Gloom Out of
Used Car Buying!

- LOW PRICES
- LATE MODELS
- LARGE SELECTION

Fiesta

OK

USED CAR
Specials!

2001

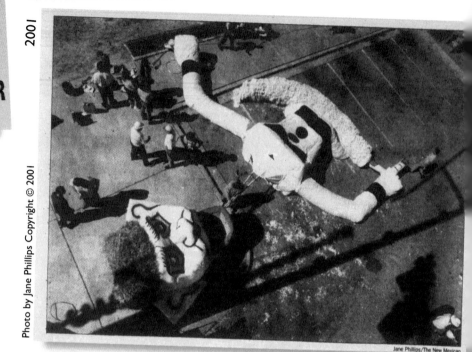

Photo by Jane Phillips Copyright © 2001

Jane Phillips/The New Mexican

1940

ZOZOBRA
Was Never Happy

HE NEVER OWNED A
CLOSSON USED CAR!

Why not join the crowd
and invest in a really good
Used Car at Clossons

These Bargains
Are
'Gloom Chasers'

1937 BUICK COUPE:
If DeVargas had
had this one he would

1984

Zozobra came to burn

1992

ZOZOBRA!

Friday, Sept. 11
Santa Fe Public Access TV 24
and KSFR 90.7 FM
present
the second annual
Zozobra Live!

A special live presentation of
the burning of Zozobra,
with portraits of fiestas
past and present.

**Only on Cable TV
Channel 24 and
simulcast on
KSFR 90.7 FM**

produced by the
Santa Fe Community College
Communications Technology Department,
Public Access TV 24 volunteers and TCI Cable in cooperation with the
Kiwanis, the Santa Fe Fiesta Council and the city of Santa Fe.

For broadcast time and information, call 438-1319.

The New Mexican Television, September 5 - September 11, 1992 - 11

1982

Hoisting the monster

The crowds come to watch
BIGGEST PUPPET
ZOZOBRA

New Mexican File Photos Copyright © 1982

in Local Newspaper

Zozobra, Santa Fe's pet monster and city icon can be found in all manner of print within the local newspaper over the years, especially during "Zozobra season." The variety shows how deeply OMG runs in Santa Fe culture. Pieces include the Burning Event itself, monster-building articles, profiles of the Fire Spirit and Gloomies of course, plus art show announcements and advertisements of all sort. But just one time, a truly sad piece: the obituary for Will Shuster Jr., Zozobra's creator. RIP Shus.

1987

1957

Photo by George Hunsley Copyright © 1957.

Zozobra meets his match in Santa Fe

1985

FREE! RED & BLUE IRON-ON ZOZOBRA®

FIESTA DE SANTA FE

GET YOURS THURSDAY, AUGUST 12TH, IN...
THE NEW MEXICAN

1976

2000

Eye for the unusual

Gallery owner **Robert Nichols** used to feature a relatively huge stable of artists exhibiting just a few ceramic pieces each, as many merchants of American Indian pottery still do. Today he represents a smaller number of artists — a core group with regular solo gallery shows.

Nichols has an eye and taste for the unusual, encouraging artists to experiment beyond traditional techniques and designs. For example, **Bill Glass**, the first non-Southwestern artist in Nichols' stable, interprets stories not of his Cherokee background but of more ancient native Mississippian cultures. His painted vessels appear almost art nouveau in style. Another of Nichols' artists, **Alton Komalestewa**, constructs rather than carves his sculptural geometric vessels.

For an overview of what gallery artists have been working on since the big push of Indian Market, a group show opens with a reception from 1 to 3 p.m. Saturday, Oct. 21, at Robert F. Nichols Gallery, 419 Canyon Road. The show hangs through Nov. 3.

M.B.

'Zozobra Figure,' 13 x 10 1/2 ceramic figurine by Janice Ortiz

ZOZOBRA PIÑATAS
"Burn Your Own"
PARTY! PARTY!
438-9343
Across From American
Home Furnishings

1994

1969

WILL SHUSTER
(Photo by Roy Rosen)

The Man Who Killed Gloom . . .

Famed Santa Fean Will Shuster Dies

A man who was at the root of Santa Fe tradition died last night. He was Will Shuster.

Mr. Shuster died at Veteran's Hospital in Albuquerque. He had been a victim of acute emphysema for many years, and was admitted last to the hospital a week ago.

He is survived by his wife Selma; two sons, Donald B. Shuster, Albuquerque; John Adam Shuster, who is working as an engineer in Bangkok, and grandchildren.

Will Shuster was an artist, and beyond that, a creator. It was he, who in the 1920s, along with four other painters, established "Los Cincos Pintores," and became a part of Santa Fe's famous art colony.

It was he who created Zozobra in the late 1920s—the famous "Old Man Gloom" whose burning begins the annual Fiesta.

Will Shuster's paintings capture the spirit of New Mexico and many are now hanging in museums throughout the country.

In a recent statement about his beliefs in art, he stated, "Art is the flowering of humanity. It embellishes life and reveals timelessly the nature of the plant on which it grew."

"Shus," as he was known, was one of Santa Fe's most beloved raconteurs. In 1966 he appeared for the Museum of

ZOZOBRA

133

The New Mexican / Mark Lenihan

OLD MAN GLOOM UP IN SMOKE — Fire and smoke signal the beginning of the end to Zozobra Friday night at Fort Marcy Park as a record crowd cheered his death.

Record crowd cheers death of Zozobra

1981

1976

1967

GLOOM GOD GROANS
Fountains of fire make Zozobra writhe in agony, signalling the end of worldly cares and the reign of joy for the 1967 Santa Fe Fiesta. Friday night's Zozobra and accompanying fireworks were among the most spectacular in the effigy's 41-year history. (Staff photo by Vina Windes)

134

Burned Out

Celebrating Zozobra's Fiery Demise

Santa Fe's daily newspaper has done a great job publishing spectacular photographs and headlines of OMG's flashy, fiery finale each year. These pages and several more that follow showcase some of the very best of these fantastical and dramatic images of a "Burned Out" Zozobra meeting his end.

Photo by Larry Beckner Copyright © 1988

1988

1994

Photo by Susan Latham Copyright © 1994

Old Man Gloom is illuminated by fireworks prior to being burned Friday at Fort Marcy park. Below, police officers Robert Ortiz, left, and Doug Atwell watch the crowd as Wesley Stallcup and Evan Powell, right, dance to music before the Zozobra ceremonies got under way.

Photos by Susan Latham/The New Mexican

Zozobra goes up in flames

THE NEW MEXICAN

The Fire Dancer taunts Zozobra, part of the Friday night spectacle of fireworks and flame at Fort Marcy Park.

The New Mexican/Juan Rios

Zozobra, Santa Fe's gloom perish in a fiery spectacle

By ED MORENO
The New Mexican Staff

Thousands cheered when the Fire Dancer committed "gloomicide" Friday.

The victim was Zozobra, a Santa Fe native who has died fiery deaths for years so that fiesta-goers will be free of gloom.

He was burned to death in Marcy Park by a choreographed pyromaniac, who was encouraged by the throng. In vain, the beast grumbled and complained about the heat, but Old Man Gloom finally perished in a conflagration unequaled in recent times.

The gloom started to vanish when the lights were doused and the ceremony began, and the fireworks raised ooohs and aaahs from the crowd. A throng had been assembling in Marcy Park for several hours, awaiting the fiery climax.

While the sunlight lasted, there was enough fried chicken to light a fire under Colonel Sanders. There also was enough beer and liquor to douse any fire, but folks seemed to be more interested in lighting their own fires while under the influence.

A child or two was lost and found. Marijuana smoke mingled with the aroma of potato salad.

An exuberant member of the audience burned a postcard of Zozobra before the sunlight evaporated.

The Fiesta spirit was brought to a high pitch as the annual Zozobra-burning kicked off a weekend of revelry. Only faint remnants of gloom remained as the overflowing crowd made its way out of the gates to waiting cars and the Plaza.

With arms flailing and rockets blasting, Zozobra was engulfed in flame while several spectators chanted, "Burn, burn, burn."

Fireworks boomed in the background when Zozobra's muslin cloak was touched off, and the fire spread slowly up his back and onto his head, where agony touched off a series of explosions behind Zozobra's eyes.

Zozobra's flailing arms began to tire, and soon they became hollow barrels of chicken wire hanging limp at his side. The bright red lips became dull black ashes on the ground.

But there was no sorrow on the grass. The crowd was obviously happier when the burning had ended. Many who were at the Zozobra burning, including hundreds of children, had never seen the annual purging of gloom. If they didn't get much out of the symbolism, they got excited about the fire

1980

Photo by Juan Rios Copyright © 1980

Zozobra meets a fiery death once again. His death frees Santa Feans from their gloom so that they may enjoy Fiesta. More Fiesta photos, Page B-6.

135

Burned Out

Day-After Reports Show Zozobra's Flaming Defeats

2001

Photo by Abel Uribe Copyright © 2001

THE SANTA FE
NEW ✦ MEXICAN
The West's Oldest Newspaper
Serving New Mexico for 152 years

The Flames of Fiesta

Zozobra, Santa Fe's Old Man Gloom, goes up in flames for the 75th time Thursday night at the Fort Marcy Complex.

Photos by Abel Uribe
The New Mexican

Fire, frivolity mark Zozobra's 75th burning

2002

ZOZOBRA
the Monster burns

Luis Sanchez Saturno/The New Mexican
The sun sets behind Zozobra at Fort Marcy Park on Thursday.

Santa Fe's annual Fiesta kicks off Thursday night with the burning of Zozobra at Fort Marcy Park. Fiesta continues through Sunday.

Top Photo by Luis Sanchez Saturno
Bottom Photo by Jane Phillips
Copyright © 2002

2003

Photo by Jane Phillips Copyright © 2003

Photos by Jane Phillips/ The New Mexican
Fire dancers entertain the crowd before the 79th Burning of Zozobra at Fort Marcy Park on Thursday evening.

In the line of fire
Gloom burns away as Zozobra is brought down in flames

Gust of flames

Zozobra-goers outlast wind delay to see Gloom's annual demise

Photo by Natalie Guillen Copyright © 2011

2011

Gloom is doomed

From left, Gabriela Romero and Esther Lesch, both 13, watch Zozobra burn.

2010

Photo by Jane Phillips Copyright © 2010

2013

Perfect burn

Photo by Luis Sanchez Saturno Copyright © 2013

2014

Zozobra ignites bigger audience

Photo by Jane Phillips Copyright © 2014

You Have to See It to Believe It

2007

Burning
of Zozobra
brings out a
city's primal
spirit

2008

A BIG BURN

for a gloomy old man

Big-Bang Endings for Old Man Gloom

2005

Photo by Lauren Clifton Copyright © 2005

2008

SORROWS SMOKED

Photo by Luis Sanchez Saturno. Copyright © 2008

From left, Myranda Chavez, 13, and Mia Melchor, 13, chant 'burn him' at Old Man Gloom. This is their fifth time watching Zozobra burn.

Watch video of the event at www.santafenewmexican.com

ZOZO'S LAST STAND

2007

Spectacular Burns
Finish Zozobra...

SLOW BURN

SANTA FE ✦ NEW MEXICAN

Locally owned and independent   Saturday, September 4, 2021   santafenewmexican.com $1.50   ★

THRILLER
97th Burning of Zozobra
SEE STORY, PAGE A-4

2021

Photo by Jim Weber. Copyright © 2021

Photo by Jane Phillips. Copyright © 2012

2012

and Banish Gloom for Another Year

2023

2022

2024

Community Catharsis

Will Shuster conceived Zozobra, also known as Old Man Gloom, as a symbolic method to dispel anxieties and doubts, reflecting his own struggles post-World War I. He shared this cathartic practice with his friends by encouraging them to write down their troubles and burn them as a means of liberation. Inspired by the Mexican tradition of burning effigies of Judas during Holy Week, Shuster integrated this practice with his own ritual of incinerating gloomy thoughts.

What sets Zozobra apart from other effigy-burning traditions worldwide is that Zozobra is neither a political nor a religious figure. Instead, he is a spectral representation of our collective worries and anxieties. Zozobra embodies our human failings, but just as we manifest him through our negative emotions, we also have the capacity to create positive energy by being selfless, generous, and loving. This positive force materializes as the Fire Spirit, Zozobra's arch enemy, who ultimately triumphs by spreading light through darkness.

The result is an annual ritual that allows people globally to symbolically burn away their troubles and gloom, merging a unique blend of personal and communal catharsis.

- Ray Sandoval

Performance Art

While Will Shuster is known as a visual artist (he was an accomplished painter after all), his greatest achievement and legacy is forever tied to his theatrical performance art piece called "The Pageant of Gloom and Joy" (aka *The Burning of Zozobra*). As a painter, Shus first and foremost wanted to "paint the night sky," which he did most successfully. He lit his monster in dramatic colors and filled the darkness around him with bonfires and shimmering, sparkling fireworks to an effect beyond what paint could ever do. Add movement and sound and you've got a phenomenal fiery fantasy in the sky. It's understandable that this grand performance piece --

encompassing visuals, music, story, dance, and puppetry -- speaks to so many people and became so accepted in the creative community of Santa Fe based on the merits of the art alone. Add in a splash of fun and revelry with the profound underlying meaning -- superficial or deeply psychological -- and this astounding work of theater becomes epic, legendary.

Sleepy Santa Fe was starting to awaken in the early 1900s. Statehood for New Mexico was achieved in 1912, and artists of all stripes were arriving to experience the traditional cultures and enchanting light of the high-altitude skies of Northern New Mexico. Appreciation

of, and support for, the arts was growing in Santa Fe. When Shuster started burning his gloomy effigy in the mid-1920s, he was in an artistic community that included scores of painters, the Museum of New Mexico (started in 1909), the rich traditions of local Hispanic and Native artists, and the burgeoning art commerce scene exemplified by the Santa Fe Indian Market (started in 1922). Over the years Santa Fe's arts community continued to grow, supporting and stimulating high-level visual and performing arts, including the Spanish Markets, the International Folk Art Market, the Santa Fe Opera, the Santa Fe Chamber Music Festival (and many others),

plus hundreds of art galleries, right up to the recent Meow Wolf arts phenomenon. The Santa Fe community culture clearly embraces arts of all type, so it is not surprising that The Burning of Zozobra would take root and grow strong in this creative environment.

The special beauty of the Zozobra performance-art event is that it was created specifically for, and attended primarily by, the local community. This event was born in Santa Fe for Santa Fe, and it represents The City Different like nothing else. As one ingredient among many in the Santa Fe arts community, Zozobra adds a unique, spicy taste to our city's flavorful cultural stew.

Fire Power

As fire consumes Zozobra in a breathtaking conflagration, the monster shakes and groans. The crowd on the field grows quiet and still, staring in amazement. Calls to *Burn Him* subside. Only the band plays on with a steady rhythm underscoring the spectacular and surreal scene unfolding before us, like a crazy dream. Eyes widen and jaws drop. Parents hold their children tighter. What a strange and powerful sight to behold: the fire prevails as flames conquer the beast, primal forces at work in the night and deep in our minds, etched into our psyche. Standing together we have faced the darkness, and our gloom is gone, for now, gone with the smoke in the night sky. Only ash remains. We win again. It was not a dream.

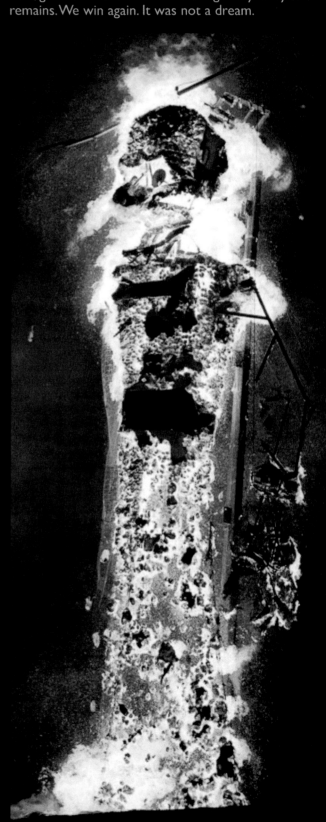

Photo Credits: Above and Opposite Page by Melinda Herrera. Right: Andres Maestas.

148

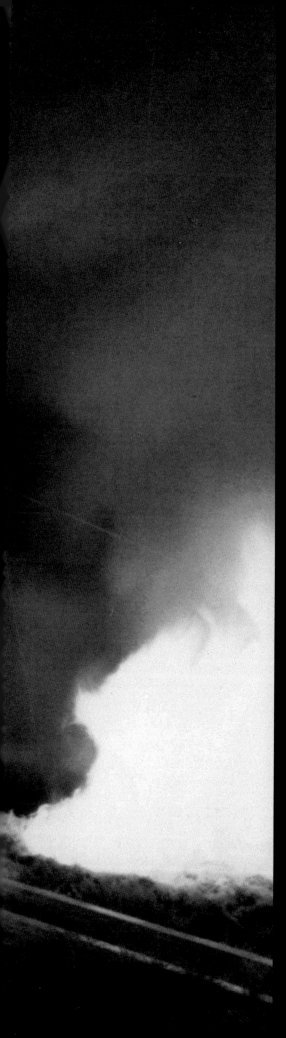

After the flames consumed the effigy,
and the embers faded into the starlit Santa Fe sky,
we stood together, a group unburdened.
In the ashes of this effigy lay the worries of the past year,
and from them, we shall rise anew,
our spirits ablaze with hope and renewal.
Tonight, we have not just witnessed a spectacle;
we have participated in a…
rite of purification, laughter, and rebirth.

- Will Shuster

151

Zozobra in Santa Fe - *How did that happen?*

Have some Faith!

The Zozobra phenomenon is so indelibly fixed in the Santa Fe experience and the psyche of (almost) all Santa Feans that it's challenging to take a step back and ask just how in the heck did this pagan-like event take hold in the City of Holy Faith?! To Santa Feans, it all just seems so natural, not even a little weird, but wonderful and fun. But... how... and why? Why here, why then?

It was perhaps a rare alignment of the stars in time and space that allowed the spark of an idea from some newly-arrived, free-spirited, creative types during the go-go Roaring Twenties to start a fire of imagination of this scale in sleepy Santa Fe. The City Different was experiencing an awakening in the nineteen-twenties with an influx of new people and new ideas. The spirit of artists and outsiders began to infuse the community with new possibilities, mixing well with the spirit of the post-WWI-1920s that leaned towards fun and gaiety over solemnity.

The New mixed with The Old in the Ancient City perched on the side of a mountain under brilliant turquoise skies. Perhaps it was their strong Faith that allowed the people of Santa Fe to build a monster of gloom each year and face that gloom, laugh at it, taunt it, stare it down, burn it down, knowing they could, knowing it would return, and having Faith that they could do it all over again next year, every year. Faith that The Fire Spirit would defeat Old Man Gloom. Faith that optimism would prevail over negativity. Faith that life goes on. And it continues to this day.

Burning a 50-foot-tall Gloom Monster each year? Why not? Meeting up with thousands of our friends and neighbors each year to yell "Burn Him" and have some fun witnessing the end of whatever gloom we need to release? Why not! Believing that we can shed the old unwanted whatever and manifest a better life for ourselves, our families, our community? Yes, of course, and why the heck not!? This is, after all, Santa Fe, The City of Holy Faith.

Photo Credits: Both Pages: All photos by Melinda Herrera

153

*Under a sky lit by
celebratory fireworks,
the flames consume Zozobra,
and he collapses at last into a
smoking pile of embers.*

*The crowd dances joyfully
as happiness and hope
return to the city and state
of Santa Fe, New Mexico.*

- Will Shuster

He is a toothless, empty-headed façade. He has no guts and doesn't have a leg to stand on.
He is full of sound and fury signifying nothing. He never wins. Every year we do him in.

- Gus Denniger, long-time Zozobrador

Muera a Zozobra!

In Santa Fe, we're all "Team Zozobra." Even those who are not big Zozobra fans and maybe haven't been to a burn for decades (or ever?!) can't deny that Zozobra has a grip on a good chunk of the population. In one way or another, Old Man Gloom is woven deep into the fabric of Santa Fe's identity, etched into our collective psyche.

A community ritual, a party, hello and goodbye. Breathe in and breathe out. "Burn Him!" then a powerful collective sigh, a sense of relief and the promise of new beginnings.

We stand shoulder-to-shoulder with our families, our friends and neighbors and strangers, young and old, tall and small, all caught up in the moment, anticipation, amazement, intention to release our troubles, if only for this one night, the joy of that feeling, conquering the beast on the hill and perhaps the sadness in our hearts and the darkness in our minds. It feels right.

We fondly look for him to appear each year, and we root for him to vanish along with our worries and cares. He's big, he's not pretty, and he's a gloomy guy, but we like him. We know he comes and goes, like our moods, like our trials and tribulations, like the weather, like the

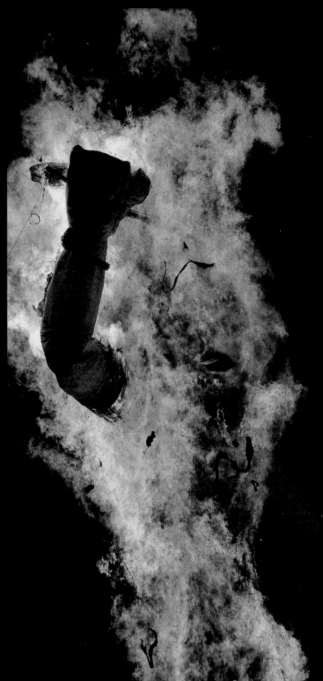

Photo Credits: Opposite Page: Both by Andres Maestas. This Page: Above Left and Below by Aaron Newsom. Above by Melinda Herrera.

pulse of our dynamic lives and the universe itself.

We know that when one Zozobra is defeated, he's not really dead. Those dark feelings will come back, and another Zozobra will too, next year, every year. And we will burn him and defeat the darkness again next year, every year. Bring him on! In Santa Fe, it's the natural order of things, like the change of the seasons, like the movement of the sun and the moon. In Santa Fe, we proudly say:

Que Viva Zozobra!

Que Viva!